ELIZABETH
CADY
STANTON

Other titles in *Historical American Biographies*

Historical American Biographies

ELIZABETH CADY STANTON

Leader of the Fight for Women's Rights

Cynthia Salisbury

Enslow Publishers, Inc.

40 Industrial Road   PO Box 38
Box 398   Aldershot
Berkeley Heights, NJ 07922   Hants GU12 6BP
USA   UK

http://www.enslow.com

*For our mother, Cynthia Salisbury. . . . Your determination
and drive not only helped you realize your dream to be an
author, but inspired us to follow ours.
Love, Mimi, Wenday, and Jen*

*Author's original dedication: To Aurelia Taylor Hostler—my
inspiration for reaching for the stars and catching them.*

Library of Congress Cataloging-in-Publication Data

Salisbury, Cynthia.
    Elizabeth Cady Stanton : leader of the fight for women's rights /
Cynthia Salisbury.
        p. cm. — (Historical American biographies)
    Includes bibliographical references and index.
    ISBN 0-7660-1616-1
    1. Stanton, Elizabeth Cady, 1815–1902—Juvenile literature.
2. Feminists—United States—Biography—Juvenile literature. 3. Women's
rights—United States—History—Juvenile literature. [1. Stanton,
Elizabeth Cady, 1815–1902. 2. Suffragists. 3. Women's rights.
4. Women—Suffrage. 5. Women—Biography.] I. Title. II. Series.
HQ1413.S67 S25   2001
305.42'092—dc21
                              2001000434

Printed in the United States of America

10 9 8 7 6 5 4 3 2 1

To Our Readers: We have done our best to make sure all Internet addresses in
this book were active and appropriate when we went to press. However, the
author and the publisher have no control over and assume no liability for the
material available on those Internet sites or on other Web sites they may link to.
Any comments or suggestions can be sent by e-mail to comments@enslow.com or
to the address on the back cover.

Illustration Credits: Enslow Publishers, Inc., pp. 11, 69, 113; Moorland-
Spingarn Research Center, p. 99; National Archives & Records
Administration, pp. 46, 52; Reproduced from the Collections of the
Library of Congress, pp. 42, 55, 60, 64, 73, 90, 97, 98, 102, 106, 109,
115; Reproduced from the *Dictionary of American Portraits*, published
by Dover Publications, Inc., in 1967, pp. 6, 27, 34, 40, 57, 67, 76, 83.

Cover Illustration: Reproduced from the Collections of the Library of
Congress

CONTENTS

Elizabeth Cady Stanton

1

A PROMISE FULFILLED

The timing was right. After a busy year spent redoing her new home and caring for her children, Elizabeth Cady Stanton welcomed the invitation she received from her old friend Lucretia Mott. It was a chance to escape her ordinary daily life, which Stanton described as "somewhat depressing."[1] Although she traveled only six miles from Seneca Falls to Waterloo, New York, to meet with Mott, the reunion put Stanton in the center of the fight for women's equality.

Eight years earlier, during the summer of 1840, Stanton had first met Lucretia Coffin Mott in Europe. The two women had made a promise: When they returned to America, they would "form a society to advocate the rights of women."[2] Although nothing had

Women's Rights in the 1800s

In most ways, women in the 1800s were considered second-class citizens. Attitudes labeled women as the weaker sex, both physically and mentally. Allowed to attend schools for boys only when there was room, girls learned to read and write in separate schools called dame schools, run by women teachers in their homes.

When a woman married, she gave up any rights she had. Laws did not allow women to vote, own property, divorce, or have custody of their own children. Women were limited to working in factories, as housekeepers, or as governesses. Occasionally, women could work as writers or teachers.

come of their plan right away, now the time had arrived to carry out their promise.

Organizing a Convention

With her personal experience as a wife and mother fresh in her mind, Stanton was ready to join the fight to end legal injustices against women.[3] When she arrived in Waterloo on July 13, 1848, Stanton joined Lucretia Mott, Mary Ann McClintock, Jane Hunt, and Martha Wright. Except for Stanton, all the women were Quakers (members of a religious group founded in England in 1652 by George Fox). Together, the women decided to organize a convention to discuss women's rights.[4]

Quakers—The Society of Friends

This religious group got its nickname, Quakers, when its founder, George Fox, was put on trial for his beliefs. Fox told the judge that he should tremble when the Lord spoke. Believing people could worship God without professional ministers, Quakers held their meetings in silence. Quakers, who believed in the equality of all people, regardless of sex or race, supported several reform causes, including temperance (limiting the use of alcoholic beverages) and abolition (the end of slavery).

Twenty-two years older than Stanton, Lucretia Mott had the activist experience Stanton did not. With the support of her husband, Mott had founded the Philadelphia Female Anti-Slavery Society. Stanton, on the other hand, had practical experience as a wife and mother.

Declaration of Sentiments

After deciding to organize a meeting for women's rights, the women moved quickly. They convinced the minister of the Methodist Church in Seneca Falls, New York, to let them hold the meeting in the church building. They also ran a newspaper notice to advertise the meeting.

On July 14, 1848, the *Seneca County Courier* ran an article announcing the convention on July 19 and 20. Its purpose would be "to discuss the social, civil and religious condition and rights of Woman."[5]

A week later, the women met again to plan the agenda for the meeting and to write a resolution on women's rights that the women in attendance could discuss. Not really knowing what to do next, the women finally found a model for their resolution—the Declaration of Independence. However, they made a few important changes. The five organizers changed the original document into a women's Declaration of Independence. Instead of demanding freedom from the king of England as the Founding Fathers of America had done, the women demanded equality for "all men and women." The opening of their declaration said it all: "We hold these truths to be self-evident: that all men and women are created equal. . . ."[6] Elizabeth Cady Stanton drafted the resolution. She called it the Declaration of Sentiments.

With the document in hand, the women prepared to host their convention. Lucretia Mott expressed some concern that, because it was harvest season, turnout might be low. But her concern disappeared on Wednesday, July 19, 1848, when "the roads approaching the Wesleyan Chapel [where the meeting was to be held] were jammed with carriages and carts. . . . More than a hundred men and women quickly filled the pews."[7] On the second day, more than three hundred women and men filled the chapel.

When the first women's rights convention was called to order, Stanton read the entire Declaration of Sentiments during the first session. Her strong words outlined the fight for women's equality. She listed the many rights women had been denied: voting (suffrage);

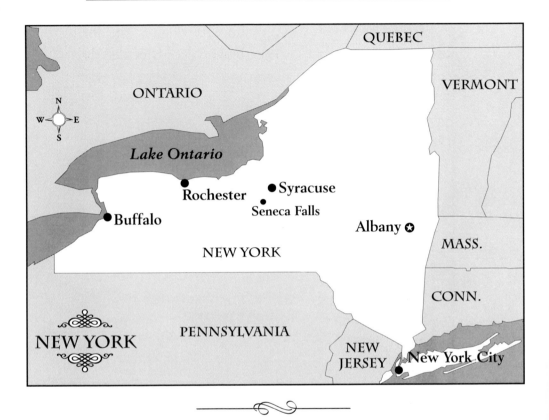

Elizabeth Cady Stanton delivered the Declaration of Sentiments in Seneca Falls, New York.

making laws; owning property; keeping earnings from a job; having custody of children; being able to divorce; earning equal wages; having equal opportunity in professions such as law, medicine, and theology; and having an equal education.

The Declaration of Sentiments, again paralleling the Declaration of Independence, ended with suggestions on how to end these injuries. The document demanded that women be given "immediate admission to all the rights and privileges which belong to them as citizens of the United States."[8] After heated words of debate for and against, the Declaration of Sentiments was adopted by the convention.

After the Convention

The *Seneca County Courier* reported on the convention's new ideas and "startling" subjects. The newspaper believed the Declaration of Sentiments would "provoke much remark."[9] The *Courier* was right. Response to the convention was largely negative. Most male newspaper editors and political figures were not yet ready to accept the idea of women starting a political movement on their own, with little help from men.[10]

However, the convention at Seneca Falls created a sisterhood of women, and despite the negative comments, it won a lot of publicity for the new movement. The Declaration of Sentiments created a new demand for equality. No longer should women's place be thought of as only in the home. Seneca Falls and the actions of Elizabeth Cady Stanton and other women's rights activists would become a model for future efforts to win women's rights in America.

2

"WHAT A PITY IT IS SHE'S A GIRL!"

Elizabeth Cady was born on November 12, 1815, in one of the finest houses in Johnstown, New York. That same year, her father, Judge Daniel Cady, was elected to represent New York in the United States Congress. As the seventh child in the Cady family, Elizabeth described herself as a "plump little girl, with very fair skin, rosy cheeks, good features, dark-brown hair, and laughing blue eyes."[1] Of the eleven children born to the Cadys, only six survived childhood: her older brother, Eleazar (born in 1806); her older sisters, Tryphena (born in 1804) and Harriet (born in 1810); Elizabeth; and her younger sisters, Margaret (born in 1817) and Catherine (born in 1819).

Surviving Childhood in the 1800s

The death of children in the 1800s was not unusual. Boys seemed more likely than girls not to survive birth and childhood illnesses. Judge Daniel Cady was devastated when he lost most of his sons as infants.

Infectious diseases such as scarlet fever, mumps, and diphtheria, which often killed children in the 1800s, would later be prevented with vaccines. Not until the twentieth century would antibiotics such as penicillin be available to treat diseases caused by bacteria.

The Cady Mansion

The Cadys' stately home towered over many of the other buildings of Johnstown. In the square, where many of the small town's activities took place, stood the school and several churches. The county court-house and jail, where Elizabeth's father spent much of his time, was directly opposite her childhood home. When Elizabeth was born, the house was wood frame. Later, it was torn down and rebuilt as a gray brick mansion.[2]

Childhood Memories

One of Elizabeth's fondest memories was of sitting by her nursery window, facing the street, and listening to farmers' wagons as they rattled over the large cobble-stone streets from morning until night. One of her favorite childhood retreats was a stream called the Cayadutta. The small river provided a place for

Founding Johnstown

Johnstown was named for Englishman Sir William Johnson, who bought the property from the Iroquois tribe before the American Revolution. Located in the southwestern part of New York State, the town was forty miles northwest of Albany. By 1815, Johnstown had a population of about one thousand people. The town claimed to be the place where the fictional American Indian hero Hiawatha lived. Poet Henry Wadsworth Longfellow made Hiawatha famous in *The Song of Hiawatha* (written in 1855). The real Hiawatha was a Mohawk chief who lived in the 1500s.

the town's children to play wading games and the power to run Johnstown's glove and steel-spring manufacturing businesses.

The Cady children spent their days playing a variety of games. In the attic, the children cracked hickory nuts, nibbled on cakes of maple sugar, chewed on dried herbs, played with the spinning wheels, and played dress-up with old clothes. When the top floor ran out of charm, the children played at the opposite end of the mansion—in the cellar, where the family stored barrels of apples, vegetables, meats, and other foods. At the end of the day, the children often carried their games upstairs, playing in the large kitchen by candlelight.

During the snowy winter months, the Cady children found fun outside. Elizabeth wrote, "we had the

snow with which to build statues and make forts. . . ."[3]
Elizabeth Cady admitted that she enjoyed outdoor
life, probably because it allowed her to escape chores
such as cleaning her room and learning homemaking
skills such as sewing and cooking.

"The Judge"—Daniel Cady

Judge Daniel Cady was the head of the household. A
guest in the Cady mansion once described the judge as
tough-minded and quiet. Elizabeth later remembered
her father as a man of firm character with unques-
tionable integrity.

Judge Cady was perhaps the most important figure
in Elizabeth's childhood. She often looked to him for
support. Sometimes, he even seemed sympathetic to
her attempts to escape household chores, and allowed
her to go horseback riding instead.

By the time Elizabeth was born, her father was one
of the wealthiest landowners in New York State. It
had not always been that way. From humble begin-
nings, Daniel Cady started his career as an apprentice
to a shoemaker.

When he lost his vision in one eye in an accident,
Cady became a schoolteacher, then went on to study
law. He moved to Johnstown in 1799. There, he met
and married Margaret Livingston.

Daniel Cady married into money. And under the
laws of the time, he acquired his wife's entire fortune
after his marriage. Judge Cady went on to increase his
family's wealth through real estate deals.

Despite his prosperity, Daniel Cady was opposed to upper-class people hoarding wealth. As a member of the Federalist political party, he believed in the right to private property. He shared Federalist beliefs that the wealthy and powerful had a responsibility to exercise control wisely and in the best interest of society.

Mother—"Queenly" Margaret Cady

Daughter of a Revolutionary War officer, Margaret Livingston Cady was twelve years younger than her husband. Elizabeth later described her mother as "a tall, queenly looking woman. . . ."[4] Margaret Cady loved living in Johnstown. She enjoyed socializing and being involved in her church.

Elizabeth wrote very little about Margaret Livingston Cady in her autobiography, making her mother appear as a minor character in her life. However, some of her mother's influence later showed in Elizabeth's life.

Margaret Cady was not easily intimidated, even by men. She was often considered to be in charge of the household. In addition to many everyday issues in which her judgment overruled her husband's, Elizabeth's mother "disagreed with [her husband's] opposition to abolition and women's rights. . . . Mrs. Cady [even] insisted that the votes of female parishioners be counted in the election of a new pastor."[5] Despite these views, which were unusual for the time, Margaret Cady still emphasized the need for her daughters to learn housekeeping and social skills more than intellectual or athletic pursuits.

A Lasting Childhood Memory

One childhood memory that left a lasting impression on young Elizabeth was the birth of her sister, Catherine. The often-told story describes how four-year-old Elizabeth was carried to the nursery to see the new baby. While in the nursery, among some family friends, Elizabeth overheard someone say: "What a pity it is she's a girl!"[6] Although little Elizabeth did not then understand the meaning of the comment, she would soon grow to realize that girls were not valued as highly as boys in American society. This realization proved to be one of the greatest disappointments of Elizabeth's childhood.

As she grew up, it seemed to Elizabeth Cady that everything enjoyable was not allowed. Some of these rules were hard on Elizabeth, who was a tomboy. The strict Presbyterian beliefs of her family sometimes seemed stern and unforgiving to a daughter who was interested in fun.

A Strict Upbringing

Elizabeth Cady's parents were traditional and very religious. Elizabeth later wrote that her parents were kind, considering the harsh religious and social customs of the time. Still, she resented the fact that she was often punished for throwing tantrums in rebellion against the strict rules of her household. She and her sister Margaret often ignored the rules, hoping to find excitement.

The Cady girls were cared for by Scottish nurses, hired by their wealthy parents to supervise the children and make sure the household rules were followed. One of the nurses once asked Elizabeth, "Child, what are you thinking about; are you planning some new form of mischief?"

Elizabeth answered, "I was wondering why it was . . . that everything we dislike is commanded by God or someone on earth. I am so tired of that everlasting no! no! no! At school, at home, everywhere it is no!"[7]

Behind their nannies' backs, Elizabeth and her sisters found ways to amuse themselves. At night, they would squeeze between the bars covering the nursery windows and look up at the stars, while their parents thought they were sleeping. Childhood became even more fun when Elizabeth finally took her younger sister's advice to do what they wanted without first asking permission from their parents. When Elizabeth expressed fear of being punished, Margaret reassured her: "Suppose we are. . . . We shall have had our fun. . . ."[8]

Great Events

Years after her childhood, Elizabeth Cady Stanton remembered the great fun she and her siblings enjoyed at special times such as Christmas and the Fourth of July.[9] Like most children, she looked forward to major holidays and vacations from school and books.

The Cady Sisters

Elizabeth's oldest sister, Tryphena, was named after their grandmother Cady. She married a clerk in her father's law office named Edward Bayard. Tryphena, who sometimes shared responsibility for her younger sisters' upbringing, did not approve of Elizabeth's later involvement with women's rights.

Harriet, the next-oldest Cady daughter, would later pay for Elizabeth's daughters' education at Vassar College. Nicknamed Haddie, she married her cousin, Daniel Cady Eaton. Although she initially supported Elizabeth's involvement in the women's rights movement, her wealthy husband made her remove her name from the Declaration of Sentiments.

Elizabeth's two youngest sisters, Margaret and Catherine, were closest to her in age and interests. Both married clerks from their father's law office. Madge and Cate, as they were called, each had five children. Both of these Cady women participated actively in the women's rights movement, alongside their famous sister.

Early on Christmas Day, with bare feet on cold floors, the children emptied their stockings. As an adult, Elizabeth Cady Stanton wrote that children growing up in later years would have laughed at what the Cady girls found in their stockings: little papers filled with candy, raisins, nuts, a red apple, and a silver quarter in the toe of the stocking (or perhaps a rock, if they had been naughty).

After they opened their Christmas gifts, Peter Teabout, one of the family's African-American servants, took the girls on a sleigh ride over snow-covered hills. Before the ride, the girls attended church with him. When they returned home, the children watched Teabout fix dinner, marveling as he flipped pancakes in the air and caught them.

Elizabeth Cady Stanton also wrote about the Fourth of July. Traditionally beginning at midnight, the people of Johnstown celebrated by lighting bonfires, cannons, and fireworks and ringing bells to welcome the patriotic day. After a parade of soldiers and towns-people, the Declaration of Independence was read. Then, a dinner was held under the trees near the old courthouse.

School Days

The Cady sisters were taught to read and write at a dame school. Maria Yost's dame school educated three generations of Johnstown children.

The sisters mastered their lessons while dressed in what Elizabeth considered extremely uncomfortable school outfits—red stockings, heavy red flannel dresses with starched ruffles at the throat, and black aprons. The uniform's starched ruffles scratched young Elizabeth's neck, but if she complained, her hand was slapped and the collar was tightened.

After Maria Yost's dame school, most of the Cady children attended Johnstown Academy. There, they made friends with the daughters of the local county sheriff and the hotel keeper. With these new contacts, they were able to visit prisoners during Court Week. The girls brought the prisoners cakes and talked to them about their crimes and punishments. With the help of the hotel keeper's daughter, they often eavesdropped on the judges and lawyers. The final excitement of Court Week was attending actual trials, hearing prisoners' arguments, and listening to the verdicts of the judge and jury.

Elizabeth once showed her unusually assertive personality during Court Week. She later wrote, "On one occasion I projected a few remarks into a conversation between two lawyers, when one of them turned abruptly to me and said, 'Child, you'd better attend to your business; bring me a glass of water.' I replied indignantly, 'I am not a servant; I am here for fun.'"[10]

During their escapades, the family servant Peter Teabout looked after the girls. It was not considered appropriate for young ladies to be out in public alone. Fortunately, their parents felt the girls were safe with Teabout. The Cady girls liked being with Teabout, who was less strict than some of their other guardians. Thanks to Teabout, Elizabeth and her sisters were often able to escape the "everlasting no! no! no!"

3

New Shoes
to Fill

Elizabeth Cady spent many hours in her father's law office. At a young age, she grew frustrated because women had few, if any, rights.[1] However, not all her time in the office was dedicated to listening to the woes of her father's clients. Judge Daniel Cady's offices were filled with law students who enjoyed teasing and debating with the judge's bright young daughter.[2] Many of these law clerks boarded at the Cady mansion. They were considered part of the family.

Unexpected Lessons in the Law

After observing Elizabeth's interest in the law, especially in regard to the rights of women, the young law clerks would tease her by reading portions of the law that made women's lives subject to the control of men. Unexpectedly, this teasing from the law students about women's inferior status gave Elizabeth Cady quite an education about women's rights. She was eventually able to memorize the parts of the law that dealt with women, after being taunted with them so many times.

Elizabeth also learned about society's discrimination against women during one well-known incident. A woman named Flora Campbell came to consult Judge Cady about a legal problem. Elizabeth listened as Campbell explained how her husband had mortgaged the farm she had inherited. Creditors were taking it over. Judge Cady explained that the law was clear—a woman's property became her husband's when they married. There was nothing he could do to help.

Elizabeth decided to take charge of the situation herself. She informed Flora Campbell that she would take scissors and cut all the laws that were unfair to women out of her father's law books. Judge Cady explained to his daughter that cutting up his books would not help, because laws could only be changed by the legislature. According to Elizabeth's later memories, her father encouraged her to write a speech that she could give to the New York state legislature when she grew up.[3]

Girlhood and Grieving

When she was barely eleven years old, Elizabeth's only brother, Eleazar, returned home for the summer after graduating from Union College. Elizabeth Cady

Stanton described him as "the pride of my father's heart."[4]

Parents in the 1800s, like the Cadys, generally preferred male children to female. Males could carry on the family's reputation and fortune. And Daniel Cady had worked hard to build an estate for his sons. As the Cadys' only son to survive to adulthood, Eleazar was the shining star of the family.

Shortly after his return home from college, tragedy struck. Eleazar fell terribly ill and died. Judge Cady was devastated.

Eleven-year-old Elizabeth later remembered how grief-stricken her father was and how she became determined to comfort him by filling the place Eleazar had left behind. She assured her father, "I will try to be all my brother was."[5]

Elizabeth Cady took her vow seriously. She immediately engaged herself in activities that were considered for boys only at that time. As fascinated as her father had once been with his daughter's bright mind and interest in the law, he seemed to lose this fascination after Eleazar died, despite her efforts to be the great success her brother might have been.

After Johnstown Academy

Elizabeth Cady attended the Johnstown Academy until she was sixteen years old. She was the only girl there who took advanced classes in mathematics and language. When it was time to go to college, Elizabeth Cady hoped to follow in her brother's footsteps and attend Union College, as she had promised her father.

Edward Bayard, a Blessing

After Eleazar died, Judge Cady replaced the loss of his son with work. After bearing another son who died in infancy, Margaret Livingston Cady had a nervous breakdown. Edward Bayard and his wife, Elizabeth's oldest sister, Tryphena, helped raise the three youngest Cady girls—Elizabeth, Margaret, and Catherine. The childless Bayards also brought life into the Cady household.

Tryphena was strict with her younger sisters, as their mother had been. Edward Bayard, however, worked hard to give the Cady girls as much fun as possible. Not only did he serve as a father figure for several years of Elizabeth's childhood, but he also gave all the Cady girls a much-needed source of loving, kind-hearted attention that was sometimes absent in their parents' serious household.

In 1830, however, most colleges did not admit women. Elizabeth Cady, whose intellectual accomplishments were as impressive as any boy's, was upset by this inequality.[6] Since Elizabeth was determined to continue her education, the Cady family decided (with the persuasion of Edward Bayard) that it would do no harm if she attended Emma Willard's Troy Seminary (an important all-girl school) in Troy, New York.

At Last, a Female Role Model

During the winter months of 1830, Elizabeth Cady began her boarding school years at Troy. She described her attitude about beginning the new school as a "hopeless frame of mind."[7] According to her memoirs, she had already studied and mastered every subject the school offered except for French, music, and dancing. However, school records show that she took many other subjects, including algebra, Greek, music, writing, botany, logic, geometry, and history.[8]

Clearly, Elizabeth missed the law clerks of her father's office who had challenged her intellectually. From that time on, she fervently advocated coeducation, believing boys provided intellectual stimulation that other girls alone did not.

Eventually, however, Elizabeth Cady found that life at Troy was not quite as bad as she expected. She liked the girls she met and the area in which the school was located. More important, when Emma Willard, the head of the seminary, finally returned from

Emma Hart Willard, a pioneer in the field of women's education, was possibly the first woman Elizabeth Cady respected greatly.

Emma Hart Willard

Emma Willard was a pioneer in the field of improving women's education. Realizing that her own education had been inferior, she became determined to help other young women avoid the humiliations she had felt when trying to understand her male relatives' and friends' books. Willard made the subjects taught at men's colleges available to the young women who attended her seminary.[9] She designed new methods to teach math and history and even wrote most of the textbooks for her students.

several months in Europe, Elizabeth Cady found a woman she admired.

Still, Elizabeth Cady continued to receive mixed messages about women's roles from the people around her. According to historian Elisabeth Griffith,

> She observed the contrast between a submissive, passive, and nonintellectual feminine ideal and the reality of an assertive, active, intelligent, and powerful female . . . [like] her mother and Emma Willard. . . . [O]ccasionally even her parents applauded intellectual accomplishment, but none of them outwardly encouraged any but traditional roles for women.[10]

A Revival

During this time, family and teachers were not the only adults who had an impact on Elizabeth Cady. Equally influential was an evangelist (a traveling

Evangelistic Preachers

Evangelists were Protestant ministers who believed that every individual needed to be spiritually reborn. The Greek translation of the word *evangelism* is "good news." The "Second Great Awakening," a religious revival that occurred during the early nineteenth century, was led by Charles Grandison Finney. (The first Great Awakening had taken place during the mid-eighteenth century.) Revival leaders were usually traveling ministers whose passionate and frightening sermons, often called "fire and brimstone," converted many members of their audience.

Protestant revival minister). Even though she had been raised in the Presbyterian Church, when Charles Grandison Finney came to Troy, Elizabeth went along with many of her classmates to hear him speak.

Elizabeth Cady Stanton later referred to Finney as a "terrifier of human souls."[11] Whatever his character, Charles Grandison Finney was able to convert scores of Americans whenever and wherever he preached.

After six weeks of listening to Finney, Elizabeth Cady found herself ready to convert. However, after publicly confessing her sins, Elizabeth Cady became so ill with worry over the fate of her soul that she had to return home to Johnstown. Her father and the Bayards took her on a trip to Niagara Falls to help her get over the nightmares she was suffering because of her experiences with Finney. Edward Bayard had her read scientific books to counter Finney's beliefs. Soon the nightmares stopped, and Elizabeth Cady was able to return to Troy to complete school.

When Elizabeth Cady graduated from Emma Hart Willard's Troy Seminary in 1833, she went home to Johnstown. Because her family was wealthy, Elizabeth Cady did not have to worry about finding a way to support herself after graduation. Instead, she spent her days going to parties and dances. She also made frequent visits to relatives' homes. It was during one of these visits that Elizabeth Cady's life took a major turn.

$\boxed{4}$

A PROMISE
NOT TO OBEY

Summer weeks spent at her cousin Gerrit Smith's home in Peterboro, New York, were very different from Elizabeth Cady's school days in Johnstown. In her memoirs, she described her cousin's home as a place filled with "love and peace, of freedom and good cheer. . . ."[1]

An Open Door to a New World

Gerrit Smith's home helped Elizabeth Cady expand her view of the world. His guests came from every part of the country—rich as well as poor. Their different backgrounds fascinated Elizabeth Cady Stanton. Gerrit Smith's father had bought land from the Oneida Indians, so members of the tribe often visited the Smiths. They felt that their land dealings entitled

Gerrit Smith

Like his cousin, Gerrit Smith had been born into money. His father, Peter, had been partners with John Jacob Astor, one of the wealthiest men in America. Together they made a fortune in fur trading and land dealings. Gerrit Smith used his fortune to promote social reform. He became a prominent abolitionist, serving as president of the New York Anti-Slavery Society from 1836 to 1839.

them to enjoy the family's hospitality. Often Smith's barn and kitchen floors made temporary homes for such visitors.

At Smith's, Elizabeth Cady also met abolitionists, temperance workers, philanthropists, and religious reformers. She learned new ideas about individual rights. "Every member of [the Smith] household is an abolitionist," she later said, "even to the coachman."[2] Gerrit Smith was also well known among runaway slaves, who knew that his house was one of the stations on what was known as the Underground Railroad, the route to escape slavery.

Lessons Learned out of School

New experiences at Cousin Gerrit's taught Elizabeth Cady about racial injustices in a way she always remembered. One day, Smith told Elizabeth Cady and her cousins that he had a secret to tell them. He asked them to follow him to the third floor. There, Gerrit

The Underground Railroad

Antislavery activists started the Underground Railroad to help slaves escape from the South to free states in the North or to Canada, where slavery was illegal. The Underground Railroad was not a real railroad. It was a group of people and houses that provided secret escape routes. The "conductors" on the railroad were abolitionists. Conductors led slaves to "stations"—safe houses where they were fed and sheltered. "Sleeping cars" were often basements, attics, barns, and kitchen floors—places where escaping slaves could safely hide along the road to freedom.

Smith introduced the girls to Harriet, an escaped slave who was being helped by members of the Underground Railroad.

Smith said, "Harriet, I have brought all my young cousins to see you. I want you to make good abolitionists of them by telling them the history of your life—what you have seen and suffered in slavery."[3] The girls listened for two hours. At sunset, dressed in the gray-and-white clothing usually worn by Quakers, Harriet left by carriage for the trip to Canada and freedom.

Later that evening, as expected, Harriet's master arrived at the Smiths' with federal marshals. Gerrit Smith invited them to dine. Over dinner, Smith explained his abolitionist views. While the dinner guests debated slavery, Harriet's carriage traveled

Elizabeth's cousin, Gerrit Smith (seen here as he looked in his later years), was one of the most famous abolitionists in the nation.

farther and farther from Peterboro. By the time the marshals resumed their chase, Harriet had a big head start.

The experience profoundly affected young Elizabeth Cady. She would spend the rest of her life fighting injustice—not only against blacks but against women.

Elizabeth Cady Gives Her Heart

The visit to Gerrit Smith's in the fall of 1839 changed Elizabeth Cady's life in other ways, too. It was there that she met antislavery lecturer Henry Brewster Stanton. She described him as "a fine-looking, affable young man, with remarkable conversational talent. . . ."[4] Ten years older than Elizabeth Cady, Stanton had come to Peterboro with a young woman, to whom most people believed he was engaged. Thinking Stanton was not available romantically, Elizabeth Cady felt comfortable around him.

Shortly after Elizabeth Cady met Henry Stanton, she had the opportunity to hear him deliver one of his extremely moving antislavery lectures, which brought

Henry Brewster Stanton
Born on June 27, 1805, in Pachung, Connecticut, Henry Brewster Stanton was the second of six children. His father was a woolens manufacturer. In 1826, his father declared bankruptcy, and the family moved to Upstate New York. Like his future wife, Elizabeth Cady, he came from distinguished ancestors—officers of the American Revolution, United States congressmen, and judges.

Stanton's first job was working on politician Thurlow Weed's newspaper. As a reward for helping Weed get elected to the New York State Assembly, Stanton was appointed the deputy clerk for Monroe County, New York. While working there, he heard Charles Grandison Finney preach. Deciding to convert, he became a strong abolitionist who demanded an end to slavery.

the audience to tears. Elizabeth Cady found Stanton attractive and interesting. She especially liked him because he did not seem to disapprove of her outgoing and politically interested personality, which many men found unbecoming in women of the time.

A Long Morning Ride

After breakfast one morning, Henry Stanton met Elizabeth Cady on the front porch of the Smith home and invited her on a morning horseback ride. Not long after, Henry Brewster Stanton proposed. Without consulting friends or relatives, Elizabeth Cady immediately accepted, grateful to have learned that the man she so greatly admired was not, in fact, engaged. Instead, he was in love with her.

Even her cousin Gerrit Smith at first opposed Elizabeth Cady's engagement to Stanton. He warned her that life with an abolitionist lecturer, whose financial prospects were often insecure, could be difficult. He also knew that her father, who thought abolitionists were too radical, would not approve.[5] Realizing that her decision to marry Henry Stanton was not going to be popular, Elizabeth Cady decided to announce her engagement by mail rather than in person. She hoped that her family's initial anger would fade by the time she saw them.

Elizabeth Cady's father was very angry. In addition, friends and relatives who had previously spoken in positive terms about marriage began to paint negative portraits of family life. All this opposition soured Elizabeth Cady's enthusiasm about her engagement. She finally decided to break it off.

Henry Stanton, however, did not give up easily. He assured Elizabeth that she would never find anyone who loved her more than he did. He wrote her many letters, assuring her of his feelings and pressing her to marry him. Stanton's letters kept the romance alive. And when Henry Stanton announced that he was going away to Europe for several months to be a delegate to the World Anti-Slavery Convention, Elizabeth Cady decided she could not wait. She had to marry Stanton now or never.

A Secret Wedding

Thinking that most members of their families would not attend, even if they were invited, Elizabeth Cady and Henry Stanton decided to keep their wedding a secret. Family minister Reverend Hugh Marie agreed to marry the couple on Friday, a day considered unlucky for marriages, rather than the traditional Saturday. After a long discussion, he even agreed to Elizabeth Cady's demand that the bride's vow to "obey" be left out of the traditional ceremony. She also decided to continue to use her own name after marriage, calling herself Elizabeth Cady Stanton, an unusual step for a married woman of the time.

On May 1, 1840, in Johnstown, New York, Elizabeth Cady married Henry Brewster Stanton. After the wedding, Elizabeth's sisters Margaret and Harriet and Harriet's husband, Daniel Eaton, accompanied the newlyweds to the dock in New York Harbor. There, the Stantons boarded the *Montreal*, the ship that would take them to England.

Off to England

The voyage took eighteen days. To keep herself occupied, the new Mrs. Stanton found companions among the ship's crew. She also spent time with James Birney, an abolitionist also on his way to the World Anti-Slavery Convention. During the long trip, Birney taught Elizabeth Cady Stanton about the antislavery movement. However, Birney's lessons went beyond abolition. As a Southerner with conservative ideas about women, he felt that Stanton was too outgoing and needed to change her ways before they landed in London.[6] He continually criticized her every move. In Birney's eyes, Stanton committed several offenses—playing tag on the deck, accepting a dare from the captain to be hauled to the top of the main mast on a chair, and even beating Birney at chess.

Elizabeth Cady Stanton wrote that Birney did not reserve his criticism for her alone. He was even more critical of her husband, who accepted and even seemed to encourage his wife's unconventional behavior.

The *Montreal* docked in London in early June. The Stantons, along with Birney, joined several other American delegates at the boardinghouse where the women representatives to the antislavery convention were also staying. Elizabeth Cady Stanton's shipboard confrontations with Birney over the status of women were just a taste of what the future would hold.

5

MARRIAGE AND MOTHERHOOD

The first World Anti-Slavery Convention opened on Friday, June 12, 1840, in London, England. Shortly after the convention was called to order, Elizabeth Cady Stanton learned that the real issue to be discussed was not slavery. The question of women being admitted to the convention was the first topic up for debate.

The issue split the delegates into two camps. Those who supported the admission of women were led by William Lloyd Garrison, a famous American abolitionist. Stanton often sympathized with the Garrisonians, as this group was called, believing women had the right to attend the convention. Her husband spoke on behalf of the women, but not as strongly as Garrison. In fact, some historians believe

William Lloyd Garrison won Cady Stanton's respect when he stood up for the outcast women delegates at the antislavery convention in London.

that, despite his speech in favor of equality, Henry Stanton actually voted against allowing women to participate in the convention.

Even though the Boston and Philadelphia antislavery societies had sent female representatives, the British convention organizers tried to make it clear that they had meant to invite only male delegates. The women, therefore, were seated in a separate railed-off part of the hall and were not allowed to speak at the convention. In protest of the women's treatment, William Lloyd Garrison sat with the banished women, despite the fact that he, as a man, was actually allowed to attend the convention. Elizabeth Cady Stanton applauded Garrison's action, and soon came to regard him as one of the foremost reformers in America, to the dismay of her husband. Henry Stanton was an abolitionist, but he supported more moderate efforts to stop slavery. Garrison, on the other hand, was a radical who demanded an immediate end to slavery in the United States. The two different philosophical outlooks made the men enemies in the abolition movement.

William Lloyd Garrison

When he was fourteen, Garrison was apprenticed to the owner of the *Newburyport Herald* newspaper. Years later, he was sued for one of his articles denouncing slavery. Garrison was found guilty and sentenced to prison. When he was released, he joined abolitionist Issac Knapp to publish *The Liberator*, which became the most influential antislavery newspaper of its time. In it, Garrison wrote articles demanding the end of slavery immediately. Threats of assassination and arrest did not stop Garrison from traveling to England to ask help from British abolitionists. Returning to the United States, he established the American Anti-Slavery Society. Later, Garrison also became an advocate for equal rights for women.

A New Friend

The first World Anti-Slavery Convention was basically a failure. Delegates did not reach agreement on any goals. The meeting was more memorable for the fights it began over women's rights than for any antislavery activity it initiated.

The convention helped Elizabeth Cady Stanton focus on the cause of women's rights. It was also at the convention that she met her lifelong friend Lucretia Coffin Mott. Lucretia Mott was one of the first women Stanton had known "who believed in equality of the sexes."[1] She wrote in her memoirs that Mott opened a whole "new world of thought" for her.[2]

Lucretia Mott (seen here in later years) became Elizabeth Cady Stanton's first inspiration and ally in the fight for women's rights.

Mott's impact on Elizabeth Cady Stanton would be enormous. Their conversations showed Stanton for the first time how a strong, independent woman could make her voice heard in the world of social reform.

The two women became inseparable. During the convention, they spent most of their free time sightseeing. Stanton was especially impressed when she had the opportunity to see her new friend preach to an audience at a Unitarian church. Stanton's new husband complained that she spent too much time with Mott—and not enough with him.

Finally, a Honeymoon

After the World Anti-Slavery Convention ended in late June, the newlyweds began their honeymoon. But Henry Stanton could not just travel. He had to give a series of forty lectures in thirty cities to pay for the trip. The Stantons spent most of this trip accompanied by James Birney and Reverend John Scoble. Scoble continually criticized Stanton's friend Lucretia Mott. Elizabeth Cady Stanton became so angry that she left the tour partway through and returned to London.

Finally, in September, the newlyweds were left alone. They took a walking tour of Scotland, then returned to London. After several farewell parties and teas, they sailed for home in December 1840. Seasick, Henry Stanton spent the whole voyage in bed while his wife read, played chess, walked the deck, and worried about the reception they would receive from her family on their return to America.

The couple arrived in New York City the day before Christmas. After staying a week with Elizabeth's sister Harriet, they headed for Johnstown in a sleigh used to deliver the mail.

Stanton's worries about her family's reception disappeared after the Cadys' warm welcome. During the newlyweds' long absence, the family had decided it was better to accept the marriage than to lose Elizabeth's affection.

After spending the next two months visiting friends and relatives, Henry Stanton finally realized that he could not support his wife on the money he made as an abolitionist speaker. Following in the footsteps of his brothers-in-law, Stanton decided to study law with Judge Cady. He hoped to get on better terms with his wife's parents and also wanted to enhance his political future. So, for the next year, he served as a law clerk in his father-in-law's office.

Elizabeth Cady Stanton was happy to be living back at home with her family. She later wrote, "These were pleasant and profitable years. I devoted them to reading law, history, and political economy, with occasional interruptions to take part in some temperance or anti-slavery excitement."[3] The knowledge gained from the various books she read would help Stanton later in life.

Elizabeth Cady Stanton also kept up correspondence with the new friends she had met in London. Her letters reflected her new interest in feminist reform.

A Family of Their Own

Only two years after arriving home from England, the Stantons started a family. On March 2, 1842, Daniel Cady Stanton, who was called Neil, was born. Two years later, Henry Brewster Stanton (Kit) was born. When both of his sons were born, father Henry Stanton was away from home on antislavery business.

Elizabeth Cady Stanton, now the mother of two, read every book she could find on child care. In reading popular theories, she found confusing and contradictory information. She decided to use the theories of Scottish doctor Andrew Combe, who advocated ideas such as giving children lots of fresh air and regulating baths with a thermometer. Most child care experts of the time dismissed Combe's ideas. Tradition called for children to be kept in nurseries closed tight against the outside air, to feed children whenever they seemed hungry, and to swaddle them, or wrap them in tight blankets and clothing to protect their growing limbs. Combe advised ignoring all these conventional notions about the care of infants.

Elizabeth Cady Stanton followed Combe's revolutionary ideas. She dressed her babies in loose clothing, allowed them lots of sunshine and fresh air, and gave them scheduled feedings rather than allowing them to eat on demand. The children's nurses and doctors fought against her ideas, but she held her ground. She knew the popular theories of the day often contradicted one another, and so she decided it was best to follow her own "mother's instinct."[4]

A Move to the Big City

When Henry Stanton passed the Massachusetts bar in October 1842, he decided to practice law in Boston. In deciding to make this move, he considered his career as a lawyer as well as his future political career. So in autumn 1843, the Stantons moved to the intellectual and reform center of the United States—Boston, Massachusetts.

Elizabeth Cady Stanton found many social, cultural, and political opportunities in the city. She attended temperance, peace, and antislavery conventions. She also enjoyed plays, concerts, and lectures. The list of guests the Stantons entertained in their new home included some of the most prominent people of the time: writers Ralph Waldo Emerson and

Nathaniel Hawthorne, poets John Greenleaf Whittier and James Russell Lowell, songwriter Stephen Foster, educator and philosopher Bronson Alcott, and abolitionist Frederick Douglass.

Frederick Douglass, a former slave and influential speaker, was one of the many celebrated personalities Stanton got to know during the years she lived in Boston.

Frederick Douglass

Frederick Douglass, an escaped slave, became an outstanding African-American speaker, journalist, and antislavery reformer. Stanton first met Douglass when she lived in Boston. By 1844, Douglass was one of William Lloyd Garrison's followers. He also traveled as a lecturer, recruiting Anti-Slavery Society members to fight for freedom and civil rights for African Americans. His autobiography, *Narrative of the Life of Frederick Douglass*, published in 1845, was a response to public criticism that he had lied about being a slave. After publication of his *Narrative* put him in the public eye, he traveled to England, fearing his former master might try to recapture him.

Returning in 1847 to Rochester, New York, he started his own newspaper, the *North Star*. In 1848, Douglass was one of the small group of men who actively spoke in support of the Seneca Falls Convention and women's rights.

While living in Boston, Elizabeth Cady Stanton learned how to run a household with a staff of servants. Her husband's career was demanding and kept him away from home almost all the time. He left his wife to take over the responsibilities of managing the home and children. Stanton took her housekeeping seriously. She took great pride in being a homemaker and mother and tried to do her best in every aspect of her domestic chores.

Two months before her thirtieth birthday, the Stantons' third son, Gerrit Smith Stanton (Gat), was born. Elizabeth Cady Stanton seemed content with her life. Her husband had begun to prosper financially. She had three healthy children, a nice home she was proud of, and many interesting friends. Henry Stanton, on the other hand, was not very content. He suffered from a chronic lung disease and had turned down the congressional nomination of the Liberty party, made up of antislavery activists, only to find out that he probably could have won.

Back to Small-Town Life

In the spring of 1847, Henry Stanton decided it was time to leave Boston. He and his family moved to the small, isolated town of Seneca Falls, New York. Elizabeth Cady Stanton was already acquainted with Seneca Falls. Her older sister Tryphena and her husband, Edward Bayard, had lived there when she was a teenager. Young Elizabeth Cady had made many long visits to see them.

At first, Stanton was happily busy, organizing her new home and overseeing repairs. But small-town living soon lost some of its charm. Seneca Falls was not the bustling, intellectually stimulating place Boston had been. The novelty of running a household had worn off, too. To make matters worse, her husband was frequently away on legal or political business, leaving her alone to handle the antics of her rowdy young sons.[5]

To top off her troubles, the Seneca Falls area sometimes had epidemics of malaria, an often deadly disease carried by mosquitoes. All the Stanton children, as well as some of the servants, soon fell victim to one such epidemic. Nursing everyone back to health while also keeping up with the constant demands of the house was a full-time job for Stanton.

For the first time, she understood why some women preferred to rest all day, even if their homes were not tidy and well organized. She found herself exhausted and wishing for a long rest.

Elizabeth Cady Stanton did not sit down and rest for long, however. Soon a cause filled any little free time she might have.

A FEW YEARS, A LOT OF CHANGE

After a year of living in Seneca Falls, Elizabeth Cady Stanton wrote about how terribly she missed big-city life and the intellectual atmosphere of life in Boston. She confided in her memoirs that she "suffered with mental hunger. . . . I had books, but no stimulating companionship."[1]

Conflicting Obligations

After the first women's rights convention, which she helped organize that summer of 1848, Elizabeth Cady Stanton's life took on a larger purpose—the fight for women's equality with men. She would quickly become one of the most famous and influential feminist leaders.

Yet Cady Stanton was not the most active or outspoken leader in the women's movement. By choice and by circumstances (the fact that she was raising three children almost entirely alone in her husband's frequent absences), she refused invitations to participate in other conventions. Because of her obligations to her family, she stayed at home in the small town she disliked.

Frustrated with her inability to take a more active role in the women's movement, Stanton tried to find a role model to show her how to balance her responsibilities at home with her public life. But she could not find anyone. Those women in the suffrage movement who did have families also had husbands who encouraged and supported their public lifestyles. Henry Brewster Stanton, despite his own reform-minded politics, did not support his wife's public life.

For twenty years after the 1848 convention in Seneca Falls, the women's movement had no single, recognized leader. Although many women, including Lucretia Mott, Lucy Stone, Amelia Bloomer, and former slave Sojourner Truth, spoke out in favor of women's rights, no one person became the undisputed head of the movement.

Stanton tried to do her part. She wrote numerous articles for reform journals as well as letters promoting the cause of women's rights. Her writing not only supported the women's movement but also helped her feel less isolated, despite living in Seneca Falls. It also prepared her for the future—when she would be able to take a bigger role in the women's movement.

Former slave Sojourner Truth preached about the rights of women and the abolition of slavery. In 1851, she delivered her famous Ain't I A Woman *speech to the Women's Rights Convention in Akron, Ohio.*

Four Mischievous Boys

On February 10, 1851, a red flag flew from the Stantons' porch, announcing the birth of another son, Theodore Weld Stanton. Hoping for a daughter, Elizabeth Cady Stanton was probably disappointed.

Henry Stanton was attending the state legislature when his fourth son was born. Having been absent for the births of all his children, Stanton was confronted by his father-in-law, Judge Cady. The judge reminded him that his family responsibilities were just as important as his public role. Taking the judge's advice, Stanton returned home.

In August 1851, the addition of a competent housekeeper named Amelia Willard helped Stanton continue her public work. During these years, she formed a committee to help improve the Seneca Falls schools and organized a coeducational gymnasium. Occasionally, when her domestic chores became unbearable, she boarded up the house and escaped to Johnstown, where, for a month or two, she could

"Young Savages"
Nine years old when his younger brother Theodore was born, Daniel (Neil) was almost as tall as his petite mother. His younger brother Henry (Kit) had a reputation for inventing both pranks and excuses. Gerrit (Gat) was five. All three boys were full of energy and mischief. Cady Stanton referred to the boys as the "young savages."[2]

enjoy the upper-class comforts and luxuries she could no longer afford.

Bloomers

By the early 1850s, Elizabeth Cady Stanton had adopted a new form of dress that made her house-keeping much easier. The new outfit, worn by many women's rights activists, was made up of long pants worn under a full skirt that came to the knees. Stanton's cousin Elizabeth "Libby" Miller had designed the garment. Stanton immediately loved it. She felt the skirt-and-pants combination opened a new world of physical activity for her.[3]

Soon, Stanton's neighbors and friends also began wearing the outfit. Amelia Bloomer, Seneca Falls' assistant postmistress and the publisher of a newspaper called *The Lily*, printed the pattern for the outfit. *The Lily*'s circulation increased, and the garment designed by Miller came to be known as bloomers.

Meeting Miss Anthony

In May 1851, Stanton had a chance meeting on a street corner that would change her life forever. Walking along the street in Seneca Falls with Amelia Bloomer, Stanton was introduced for the first time to the woman who would become her partner in the struggle for women's rights—Susan B. Anthony. Stanton later wrote: "There she stood with her good, earnest face and genial smile, dressed in gray delaine [cloth], hat and all the same color relieved with

Election Day!

This cartoon captured a common anti-suffrage concern: If women got the right to vote, they would no longer want to stay at home.

Susan B. Anthony

At age fifteen, Susan Brownell Anthony (the second of eight children) became a teacher to help her family financially. Earning one fourth of what male teachers earned, she came to resent the treatment of women in American society. Before meeting Elizabeth Cady Stanton, Anthony fought for temperance and the abolition of slavery, but she still felt dissatisfied, as if she needed to take action. After meeting Stanton in 1851, Susan B. Anthony began working energetically for women's rights.

Anthony and Stanton, despite the drastic differences in their lifestyles—Anthony was a single woman with freedom to travel and lecture, while Stanton was a stay-at-home mother—the two women formed a friendship that would endure for the rest of their lives.

pale-blue ribbons, the perfection of neatness and sobriety. I liked her thoroughly."[4]

Stanton soon asked for Anthony's help in the feminist cause. The strengths of each woman supported the other. The two developed a friendship and partnership. Together, they composed eloquent speeches and articles on a number of reform causes, including temperance and abolition, but they focused especially on women's rights and suffrage.

Stanton, who had a keen mind and an eye for detail, provided the ideas, words, and strategies. Anthony, who had a strong presence and the freedom

Susan B. Anthony (seen here in her seventies) would become Stanton's greatest friend. For decades, the two women would maintain a productive partnership within the fight for women's rights.

to travel widely, delivered speeches, passed around petitions, and rented buildings to hold meetings. As Stanton put it, "I forged the thunderbolts, she fired them."[5]

When Elizabeth Cady Stanton became overwhelmed with the conflicting responsibilities that went with being both a mother and an activist, Anthony sometimes came to live with the Stantons. She helped Stanton with her domestic chores to allow her friend time to research and write on behalf of the women's movement. Susan B. Anthony continued to encourage her friend to be more involved in public life. Together, they worked hard for women's rights.

In 1852, Stanton wrote a speech that Anthony delivered at the Third National Women's Rights Convention. In it, Stanton expressed some radical ideas. The speech proposed that, because women did not have the right to vote, they should refuse to pay taxes. The speech also encouraged women to seek coeducational opportunities and to oppose church leaders who refused to support equal rights for women.

Fifth and Final?

On October 20, 1852, Stanton happily flew a white flag at her home, announcing the birth of a daughter. Again, Henry Stanton was away from home. Elizabeth Cady Stanton named her first daughter after her mother, Margaret Livingston Stanton. A few weeks after Margaret's birth, Stanton wrote that this would be her last baby. She was tired of managing the household so often without her husband, while also trying to fulfill Susan B. Anthony's frequent speech-writing demands.

In February 1854, Stanton focused her attention on preparing for the first meeting of the Woman's Rights Association of New York. The women at the convention decided to present their case for equal rights to the New York Legislature and chose her to give the speech. She accepted. With Susan B. Anthony's help, Elizabeth Cady Stanton wrote her speech.

Speech Before the Legislature

Stanton knew the speech was important. In her memoirs, she devoted a whole chapter to her "First Speech Before a Legislature."

On her way to Albany, where the legislature met, she stopped at Johnstown to see her family. That evening, alone with her father in his office, she read her speech. Her father's eyes filled with tears. According to Elizabeth Cady Stanton, he said, "Surely you have had a happy, comfortable life. . . . one might naturally ask, how can a young woman, tenderly brought up, who has had no bitter personal experience, feel so keenly the wrongs of her sex? Where did you learn this lesson?"

"I learned it here [at home]," she responded.[6]

Together, the two worked on revising the speech until one o'clock in the morning.

Other versions of this story contradict Stanton's memory. Apparently, when Judge Cady read in the newspaper that his daughter was planning on giving a

The press continued to make fun of women's rights workers for their so-called "manly" behavior, but most suffrage leaders realized that even negative publicity could ultimately help their cause.

speech to the legislature, he warned her not to follow through with her intention. He believed it would embarrass the family. He threatened to write her out of his will if she went ahead with the speech. It seemed he had forgotten that it was he who had encouraged Stanton to speak before the legislature when she was a child visiting his law offices.

On February 14, 1854, Elizabeth Cady Stanton stood before the New York State Legislature. Susan B. Anthony supported her friend by printing fifty thousand copies of the speech. She put a copy on the desk of every legislator and passed the other copies out all over the state.

Stanton spoke about the inequalities of women as wives, widows, and mothers. She asked the legislators to allow women to get an equal education, to earn or inherit money and land, and to vote. She also asked that mothers be granted the right to share the custody of their children and to be protected against abuse by their husbands.

Facing Her Critics

When Stanton was criticized for leaving her children at home to speak to the legislature, she became more and more resentful of marriage and her own husband, who continued to oppose her public activity. Henry Stanton's frequent absences made it hard for her to travel to women's rights events. Although she was often asked to attend conventions as a suffrage leader, she usually had to stay home to care for her home and her children. So, in the mid-1850s, Elizabeth Cady Stanton stepped out of the spotlight. The cause for women's rights was again left without one of its strongest leaders.

7

A SPLIT IN THE CAUSE OF EQUALITY

Elizabeth Cady Stanton's speech to the New York State Legislature in Albany did not result in any immediate changes in state law. However, it struck a chord in the minds of legislators, who had already passed a law allowing married women to own property. Eventually, the state legislature would vote to grant other rights to women in New York.

For a while, Stanton stayed true to her decision to remain at home, refusing invitations that took her away from her children. She focused mainly on writing and raising her family.

To keep her bright and active mind busy, Stanton again sent articles to journals and newspapers and wrote lectures for others to present at public gatherings. She regularly contributed to *The Lily*, Amelia

Bloomer's monthly magazine, which had been an advocate of temperance before becoming the first publication dedicated to women's suffrage.[1] She also wrote monthly essays for *Una*, a paper whose main purpose was to raise the status of women. When *The Lily* was sold and *Una* stopped publishing, Stanton continued to write, sending articles to newspapers such as the *New York Tribune*.

On her fortieth birthday, Stanton probably hoped her family was complete, especially since she had already given birth to the daughter she wanted. She planned to return to the women's rights cause as soon as her youngest child, Margaret, was walking. Her plans changed when she found out she was pregnant again.

On January 20, 1856, Stanton gave birth to a second daughter, Harriot Eaton Stanton. For Stanton, becoming a mother for a sixth time seemed to be a terrible interruption. She wrote to a friend about her disappointment with the delay in returning to giving lectures. Unlike most other suffragists, not only did Stanton have to balance her own responsibilities, but she also had to win over her family, who opposed her return to public life.

Who Is Leading the Fight?

By 1857, many of the women leading the fight for women's equality were busy raising families. Susan B. Anthony, who remained single and devoted herself wholeheartedly to the cause, was left alone, a fact she often resented. Many others involved in the women's

Elizabeth Cady Stanton was frustrated after she continued to give birth to more children, which kept her from working full-time for women's rights. She is seen here with her daughter Harriot.

reform movement were also busy with antislavery issues, which were becoming more important as relations between the North and the South grew worse because of disagreements over slavery and states' rights. With few strong supporters for women's rights, money became a problem. No donations meant no way to continue the fight.

Even with these temporary hurdles, the women's movement made progress. Ohio and New York passed laws allowing women to own property. The Wisconsin and Nebraska legislatures brought up for consideration laws that would give women the right to vote. Some colleges were now admitting both men and women.

Motherhood—Again

Then came another surprise. Stanton found out that she was pregnant for the seventh time. The Stantons' last child, Robert Livingston Stanton, was born on March 13, 1859. At the age of forty-three, Stanton found this pregnancy very difficult. She wrote to Susan B. Anthony, "you need expect nothing from me for some time. I have no vitality of body or soul. All I had or was has gone with the development of that boy."[2]

Stanton's disappointment at her continued forced absence from public life was evident. Adding to her depression over her slow recovery after childbirth was the death of her father, Judge Daniel Cady, about six months later. Despite her father's frequent threats of disinheriting her during his life, he actually left his outspoken daughter around fifty thousand dollars. The

money was a welcome addition to the family income, since Henry Stanton's salary was rarely enough to support the household.

Back to Life in the Public Eye

When Susan B. Anthony volunteered Elizabeth Cady Stanton to give three speeches in 1860, she agreed. By this time, her husband was busy working for the upcoming Republican presidential election. Most of their children were in school. The older boys were almost grown. And her father's inheritance had given her enough financial freedom to travel.

After a three-year break, Elizabeth Cady Stanton jumped right back into the cause, giving three speeches in one month. On May 6, 1860, she spoke before the New York Legislature in Albany in favor of an amendment to the Married Women's Property Act. On May 8, she spoke for women's suffrage before the American Anti-Slavery Society in New York City. Then, on May 11, she defended divorce reform at the National Women's Rights Convention.

This last issue was an especially controversial one. Even many people who supported women's right to vote did not want to see freer attitudes toward divorce take hold. When Stanton made public her liberal views on divorce, it caused a scandal. Her outspokenness, however, did lead to some changes. The state of Indiana passed a liberal divorce reform bill, adding to the existing grounds for divorce desertion, drunkenness, cruelty, and adultery.

When asked to speak before the New York Legislature, Elizabeth Cady Stanton gladly accepted. She wanted to speak publicly about her ideas on divorce to show other women that they should not have to suffer needlessly in an abusive or otherwise unhappy marriage. She hoped they could one day use divorce reform laws to win control over their lives. The day after Stanton's speech, the amendment to the Married Women's Property Act passed. With this success, Stanton decided to make divorce the subject of her speech to the Tenth National Women's Rights Convention.

Two days after speaking to the legislature, Stanton presented resolutions in favor of divorce to the Anti-Slavery Society. Later, she wrote that she was shocked and upset when her ideas were challenged by a man she admired. Twenty years before, Wendell Phillips, an ally of William Lloyd Garrison, had defended the equality of women delegates at the World Anti-Slavery Convention. Now, he was calling Stanton's ideas about divorce reform irrelevant.

Despite their years as colleagues in the fight against slavery, Wendell Phillips was an outspoken critic of some of Stanton's more radical ideas.

Susan B. Anthony tried to defend her friend Stanton by saying that marriage had always been unfair to women, who basically became the property of their husbands. Despite this support, Stanton's resolutions were defeated when put to a vote. Stanton later reflected that the defeat was not caused by any failure on her part or by any flaw in her resolutions. Rather, she believed, the proposals had failed because most people had simply not been ready to accept what were then seen as radical new ideas.

A Move to New York City

Elizabeth Cady Stanton's focus on divorce reform faded as the 1860 presidential election drew near. Hoping to win a president-appointed position, Henry Stanton served as a delegate to the Republican National Convention. He supported the candidate who lost the nomination, but both Henry Stanton and Elizabeth Cady Stanton were happy when Republican Abraham Lincoln won the general election.

To his surprise, Henry Brewster Stanton did receive a political appointment, as a New York City Customs House collector. The entire family looked forward to the move. Finally leaving small-town life behind, they arrived in New York City in spring 1862.

Two Friends, Two Views

By the time the Stantons moved to New York City, the Civil War—fought because differences between the North and the South over slavery and states' rights had led the Southern states to leave the Union—had begun. Elizabeth Cady Stanton supported the North's effort to force the South, which now called itself the Confederacy, back into the Union. Susan B. Anthony opposed the war. Her opposition was not based on religious beliefs or pacifism (opposition to settling differences through violence). Instead, she thought the war would set back the fight for women's rights by focusing reform efforts exclusively on slavery, taking women's rights out of the spotlight.

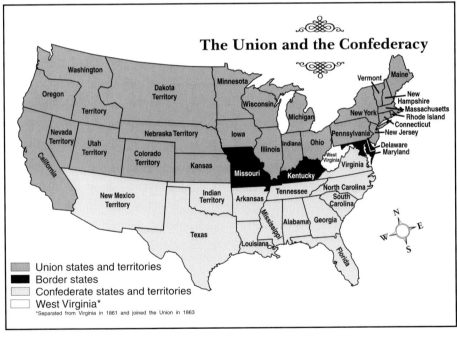

The Civil War was fought between the Union and the Confederacy. Stanton supported the Union's war effort, hoping to show how great the contributions of women could be to society and government.

Elizabeth Cady Stanton was actively involved in the war. Unlike Anthony, she thought it would help the fight for women's equality. Stanton believed men would see women actively and competently helping the war effort and would realize they deserved equal rights. This was the first time the two friends had disagreed over a major issue.

Eventually, the two resolved their differences. Stanton and Anthony again joined forces, creating the National Woman's Loyal League to work for abolition and women's suffrage. The league collected signatures in support of the passage of the Thirteenth Amendment,

Women in the Civil War

Women played diverse roles—both in the North and the South—during the Civil War. Many served as nurses, tending the sick and wounded soldiers of both armies. Others worked as spies, relaying vital information to military and political leaders. Some women even donned men's clothing and headed off into battle themselves.

Besides these support roles, women in the Civil War also served as organizers and executives. They founded the United States Sanitary Commission, a voluntary organization that helped sick and wounded soldiers. Women also established the first national women's political organization, called the Woman's Loyal League. As founders and executives of war-related organizations, women broadened their role and helped promote the cause of the women's rights movement.

which would free all slaves permanently. When the organization dissolved in 1864, it had collected four hundred thousand signatures in support of the Thirteenth Amendment, which would actually be added to the United States Constitution in December 1865, several months after the North won the Civil War.

When the Civil War ended in 1865, Reconstruction—a period during which the Southern states were brought back into the Union—began. In 1869, Stanton and Anthony founded the National Woman Suffrage Association (NWSA). It was formed to make women's rights the major focus of reform movements across America.

During and just after the Civil War, many reformers were focusing their attentions on gaining rights for former slaves and protecting African Americans from violence at the hands of racist whites, especially in the South. Some reformers referred to the Reconstruction period as the "Negro's Hour," declaring that it was important to secure African-American rights firmly before attempting to win new rights for women as well.

Stanton and Anthony staunchly disagreed with this attitude. Reminding political leaders of women's contributions during the war, they demanded that their rights be considered alongside, if not before, those of former slaves. At times, some reformers, including Stanton and Anthony, even seemed to take on a racist tone. They claimed that well-educated, intelligent white women were more deserving of the vote and

Civil War Amendments

After the Civil War, three amendments were added to the Constitution to protect the newly won rights of the former slaves. No provisions, however, were made to grant the same rights to women.

The Thirteenth Amendment

Section 1. Neither slavery nor involuntary servitude, except as a punishment for crime whereof the party shall have been duly convicted, shall exist within the United States, or any place subject to their jurisdiction.

The Fourteenth Amendment

Section 1. All persons born or naturalized in the United States, and subject to the jurisdiction thereof, are citizens of the United States and of the State wherein they reside. No State shall make or enforce any law which shall abridge the privileges or immunities of citizens of the United States; nor shall any State deprive any person of life, liberty, or property, without due process of law; nor deny to any person within its jurisdiction the equal protection of the laws.

Fifteenth Amendment

Section 1. The right of citizens of the United States to vote shall not be denied or abridged by the United States or by any State on account of race, color, or previous condition of servitude.[3]

other constitutional rights than were uneducated former slaves.[4]

More conservative feminists, who opposed Stanton and Anthony's attitude of urgency for women's rights, decided to create their own organization. It was called the American Woman Suffrage Association (AWSA). For many years, the cause of suffrage would be split

The National Woman Suffrage Association (NWSA) was started in 1869 to support some of the more radical ideas advocated by Elizabeth Cady Stanton.

between these two groups, who seemed to find it impossible to unite.

The Struggle Continues After the War

At its first meeting after the war, the National Woman Suffrage Association invited the leaders of the American Anti-Slavery Society to join to form the American Equal Rights Association (AERA). Stanton and Anthony explained how the fight for suffrage for African Americans and women could then be changed to demand universal suffrage.

The Fifteenth Amendment guaranteed voting rights to freed male slaves. In passing it, Congress had been specific in its opposition to giving women the vote. Discouraged, Stanton and Anthony turned away from resolving women's issues on the national level. Instead, they tried to convince the New York State Constitutional Convention to support women's suffrage. This new strategy focused on the states. Some suffragists believed full rights could eventually be won state by state, especially considering Congress seemed unwilling to consider a national constitutional amendment. As more states gave women the right to vote within their borders, the other states—and eventually, the nation as a whole—would have to follow suit.

When the attempt to win suffrage in New York failed, Stanton and Anthony focused on Kansas, which was also considering a suffrage amendment. They campaigned throughout the state to support the amendment. The two endured terrible roads and food and even insects in the rooms they slept in. For

Stanton, the trip showed her that she could withstand physical hardships, despite her background as the daughter of a wealthy family. The experience improved her self-esteem.[5] Despite their efforts and sacrifices, however, the suffrage amendment was defeated.

The Revolution

While in Kansas, Stanton and Anthony met George Francis Train. He would play a vital role in the next stage of their partnership. Train was a controversial figure. A millionaire who liked to dress lavishly, he was also a political radical who hoped to become president someday. Train supported women's suffrage, but many people believed it was more because he hoped women would use the vote to elect him president than because of any fervent belief in the equality of the sexes. Many people also considered Train a racist.

Despite his strange ways and the negative view many reformers held of him, Stanton and Anthony were grateful to accept Train's financial support for their cause. The Kansas trip had been a terrible failure, and the women were eager to find someone so willing to embrace women's suffrage.

Train offered to finance a newspaper to be run by the two activists. Stanton and Anthony named their journal *The Revolution*. Stanton chose the name because she considered Reconstruction another American Revolution. This revolution, she hoped, would result in the liberation of women, as well as African Americans. The first issue was published on

Stanton was grateful for the outspoken support of George Francis Train, despite his eccentricity and sometimes offensive behavior.

January 8, 1868. Its six pages were written mainly by Stanton.

"Men their rights and nothing more; women their rights and nothing less," was *The Revolution*'s motto.[6] In this journal, Stanton finally had a way to publicize even her more radical ideas, such as divorce reform and sexual freedom. In its pages, Stanton helped launch an era of militant suffragist activity, attacking men for their tyranny over women: "The male element is a destructive force, stern, selfish, aggrandizing, loving war, violence, conquest, acquisition, breeding in the material and moral world alike discord, disorder, disease, and death. . . ."[7] Anthony, on the other hand, looked at *The Revolution* as a starting point for the eventual establishment of a journal run exclusively by women, although she and Stanton appreciated George Francis Train's financial assistance while it lasted.

While Stanton and Anthony were thrilled with their great new opportunity to spread their views in a women's suffrage paper, many of their fellow suffragists looked with disgust at *The Revolution*. Not only was the character of its cofounder, George Francis Train, in question, but it was also controversial for its radical content. Some suffrage leaders feared *The Revolution*'s obvious hostility would prevent men—especially working-class men—from ever lending their support to the cause of women's voting rights. It must be remembered that, although the suffrage movement was led by women, it required the support—and the votes—of men in legislatures around the country to win its goals. So suffrage leaders spoke out against Stanton and Anthony's criticisms against men, and especially their opposition to the Fifteenth Amendment to the Constitution, which gave African-American men, but not women, voting rights. Other suffragists believed *The Revolution*'s outspoken comments might scare away former abolitionists—who might well be the women's best allies in the fight for suffrage.

The controversy turned out to be short-lived. After only two and a half years, George Francis Train withdrew his financial support from the paper. *The Revolution* was forced to stop publication.

Becoming a Radical

In such efforts as *The Revolution* and her fight to stop the Fifteenth Amendment, it seemed that Elizabeth Cady Stanton was distancing herself from other feminists. She refused to admit men into the NWSA and campaigned for the rights of working women. She associated with unwed mothers and advocates of free love. These controversial actions further alienated many leading suffragists. By 1870, she had not only lost the fight for most causes she believed in (property rights for married women, divorce reform, and suffrage), but she often stood alone with her radical reform views. Even her friend Susan B. Anthony often disagreed with her positions, although she usually tried to defend Stanton whenever possible.

In 1868, Elizabeth Cady Stanton bought a house in Tenafly, New Jersey, with some of the inheritance money her father had left her. In making this move, Stanton was demonstrating that she could make big decisions without her husband's input. For the first time in their married life, it was Elizabeth Cady Stanton—not Henry—who chose where the family would live. Now that the children were older, Stanton had some of the freedom she had always yearned for. She could spend most of her time with Anthony, forging ahead in the fight for equality for women.

8

ON THE ROAD

Stepping into a role once reserved for men only, women began to join the lyceum, or lecture, circuit in the late 1860s. Before radio and television, speakers on tour provided audiences throughout the United States with a way to learn about major issues of the day. Lyceum topics changed greatly after the Civil War. Instead of arguments about slavery, states' rights, and the role of African Americans, audiences now wanted to hear about the changing role of women and the future of women's rights.

Hardships on Friendship

Trying to win support for women's suffrage, Elizabeth Cady Stanton and Susan B. Anthony joined the lyceum circuit. A New York agency arranged their schedule. Following the path of the new railroads, Anthony and Stanton traveled as far as California.

The lyceum circuit became very popular and attracted a variety of speakers, from journalists to generals. With the opening of the transcontinental railroad in May 1869, the lyceum circuit could reach from coast to coast. Speakers traveled faster than ever before to states across the nation.

Stanton enjoyed the lecture circuit. She felt it gave her an opportunity to educate Americans about the important issues of the day. Unlike Anthony, Stanton did not limit her speeches to the subject of women's suffrage. Instead, she spoke on more personal issues such as birth control, marriage, and religion.

Their joint lecturing trip did not provide the bonding experience the two friends had expected. Although they had pleasant moments, Stanton and Anthony had disagreements, most of them personal. Susan B. Anthony nagged Stanton about her increasing weight. Anthony also seemed jealous of the attention Stanton received.[1]

Controversy between the two old friends continued throughout the trip. Finally, the two women went their separate ways. Anthony continued to give lectures. She wrote that she missed her friend, but she sometimes seemed to enjoy having the spotlight to herself.

When she learned that her mother was seriously ill, Elizabeth Cady Stanton left the speaking tour and went to Johnstown. She stayed with her mother until Margaret Livingston Cady died a week later.

The Lyceum Circuit
Inspired by James Redpath, an abolitionist and Civil War newspaper correspondent, the Lyceum Bureau brought entertainment and education to small towns throughout the United States. In rural western areas, most lyceum speakers appeared in areas that had few libraries or theaters. The Lyceum Bureau took care of scheduling the speakers, arranging their trips, and advertising the tours. Speakers were paid between one hundred and two hundred dollars for a performance. The bureau deducted its expenses and took a 10 percent commission for its staff.

After the funeral, Cady Stanton returned to New Jersey. There, she was busy getting her youngest children ready to start school for the year. She did not rejoin Anthony on the lecture tour. In fact, ten years passed before Anthony and Stanton traveled together again.

Testing the Constitution

Elizabeth Cady Stanton joined her husband during the summer of 1872 to engage in politics. Both Stantons had been asked to campaign for Republican presidential candidate Ulysses S. Grant. Although Stanton was not very enthusiastic about Grant's candidacy, she decided to support him and the Republican party because their platform—unlike the Democrats'—included women's suffrage.

That same year, hoping to win publicity for the NWSA, Stanton's old friend Susan B. Anthony decided to try a radical act. Hoping to test her theory that women already had the right to vote under the Fifteenth Amendment, which mentioned race but not sex, Anthony and one hundred fifty other women across the United States voted in the 1872 presidential election. Local officials, afraid of what the women might do if they were sent away, allowed them to cast their ballots. Anthony was promptly arrested. Tried and found guilty, she was fined one hundred dollars for voting illegally.

Elizabeth Cady Stanton did not support her friend before, during, or after the trial. While visiting her family in Peterboro and Johnstown, Stanton even passed near the courtroom when Anthony's trial was in session, but did not stop. Although she defended the judge's decision in the case, denying that women already had the right to vote, Stanton did write several articles explaining the constitutional argument behind Anthony's action.

Victoria Woodhull and More Problems in the Movement

When women's rights leader Victoria Woodhull was arrested in 1872 for sending obscene material through the mail, she decided to strike back at her opponents. In so doing, she caused a scandal that would change the women's movement forever.

Rather than deny the charges against her, Woodhull called those who had accused her of improper behavior

Henry Ward Beecher's public quarrel with Victoria Woodhull would cause many problems for the suffrage movement, and especially, the reputations of Elizabeth Cady Stanton and Susan B. Anthony.

hypocrites. She then accused famous minister Henry Ward Beecher of having an affair with a woman named Elizabeth Tilton, a member of his church. Controversy arose in the women's movement when Woodhull named Elizabeth Cady Stanton as her source for the allegation against Beecher.

Though most suffragists avoided association with Woodhull, both Stanton and Anthony supported her.[2] Stanton, who claimed that Woodhull had misquoted her, never actually denied the story. Most historians believe that Stanton did, in fact, know about Beecher's affair with Tilton. Beecher, however, took offense to the charge and set out to clear his name by attacking those who seemed to be opposing him—the suffragists.

Beecher published an article that named Victoria Woodhull, Elizabeth Cady Stanton, and Susan B. Anthony as supporters of free love, or promiscuous sexual activity. Beecher's popularity and his negative comments about key women's leaders hurt the suffrage movement greatly. Stanton was outraged when Beecher was cleared of the charges against him, especially considering that she and her associates had been left with a reputation for radical beliefs that would be damaging for years to come. After the Beecher incident, Stanton refused to take public stands on how she viewed the issues surrounding controversial trials. She also drifted away even more from her old friend and partner, Susan B. Anthony.

A New Declaration

Elizabeth Cady Stanton returned to the lyceum circuit as a regular speaker. Each January, she left home to tour. When she returned home at the end of May, her children were out of school for the summer. In the fall, after school started, she toured again for three more months.

Elizabeth Cady Stanton's lyceum schedule was a demanding one for a woman in her fifties. Circuit speakers traveled in some of the most bitter winter temperatures and conditions. From being stranded for hours on the Mississippi River because of ice to a six-hour sleigh ride through snow and wind, Stanton endured many inconveniences. Meanwhile, she was becoming a celebrity who was often asked for her autograph.

Occasionally, Stanton took a break from her lecture schedule to attend conventions of the NWSA. Susan B. Anthony, as president of the association, decided that a new Declaration of Women's Rights should be written for the one-hundredth birthday of the United States, which would be celebrated in Philadelphia on July 4, 1876. Anthony had in mind the perfect person for the job—Elizabeth Cady Stanton. But the two friends were still out of touch after their last major disagreement. Anthony, therefore, sent suffragist Matilda Gage to ask Stanton to compose the declaration. At first, Stanton refused. Eventually, however, she either realized that she was indeed the best available person to write the document, or possibly she realized the historic importance of the event. Elizabeth Cady Stanton finally changed her mind and accepted the invitation.

The Fourth of July celebration was filled with exhibits, speeches, and parades. President Ulysses S. Grant spoke at the opening ceremony. When the NWSA requested space to put up an exhibit, it was refused. Not wanting to be left out, the group built its own "Women's Building."

When the women arrived at the main events in Philadelphia, their request to be a part of the ceremony was refused. So, Susan B. Anthony decided that she, along with four other suffragists, would simply crash the party. Interrupting the chairman of the centennial event, the women marched into Independence Hall and presented their declaration, distributing copies of the document to the audience as they left.

Although the declaration attracted publicity, it was mostly negative. Disappointed, Elizabeth Cady Stanton came to believe that the main focus of the women's struggle should be on passing a nationwide constitutional amendment that would give women the right to vote. The NWSA collected ten thousand signatures in support of such an amendment. As president of the NWSA, Susan B. Anthony presented the signatures to the United States Senate, but the male members did not take the petition seriously. In fact, according to one newspaper report, "the entire Senate presented the appearance of a laughing school practicing sidesplitting."[3]

President of the NWSA

At the national convention of the NWSA in 1877, Susan B. Anthony stepped down as president. Elizabeth Cady Stanton took her place. Behind the scenes, however, Anthony continued to be in charge. Because Stanton was the better speaker, the two agreed that Stanton should maintain control of the podium. Anthony and Stanton had found a way to reestablish their partnership.

After organizing the 1878 NWSA National Convention in Washington, D.C., Elizabeth Cady Stanton left on her annual lecture tour. At the age of sixty-three, the lecture tour was becoming more difficult. To add to the hardships of the circuit, in 1878, Stanton had an accident while on tour. The omnibus she was riding in overturned, leaving her with an injured leg and back. Then, in the fall of 1879, she caught pneumonia. Probably these events, combined with her age, helped her make the decision to retire from the lyceum circuit. However, Stanton would find other ways to remain active in the women's movement.

9

HELLOS AND GOOD-BYES

On November 12, 1880, Elizabeth Cady Stanton, now sixty-five years old, started keeping a diary. One of her first entries was about the death of her friend, Lucretia Mott, who had encouraged Stanton to write a history of the women's suffrage movement. About a week after Mott's death, Susan B. Anthony and Matilda Joslyn Gage joined Elizabeth Cady Stanton to begin the massive project. The trio signed partnership papers. Gage and Stanton agreed to collect the resources and write the history. Meanwhile, Anthony would do research and secure a publisher for the volumes.

In November 1880, the three women met at Stanton's home in Tenafly, New Jersey, to begin. They used several sources: personal memories, biographical materials, photographs, speeches, newspaper articles, and their own files. Anthony and Stanton argued about what the volumes should contain, but they managed to resolve their differences without harming their friendship, as had happened in the past.

The first volume of *The History of Woman Suffrage* was finished in six months. In May 1881, Cady Stanton wrote that it was published "with good paper, good print, handsome engravings, and nicely bound."[1] It received better reviews than Stanton had anticipated. At 871 pages, the volume recorded the events of the women's movement from 1848 to 1861.

Taking most of the summer off to put on a series of women's rights conventions, Anthony and Stanton started work on the second volume of the *History* at the end of October 1881. Progress on the second volume stopped when Elizabeth Cady Stanton came down with malaria. With the help of an inheritance Anthony received from a Boston reformer, and with Stanton's daughter Harriot helping to edit, research, and write, volume two (covering the years 1861 to 1876) was finally finished in May 1882.

Mother and Daughter Take a Vacation

With volume two completed, Elizabeth Cady Stanton and her daughter Harriot departed for Europe. After the two visited Stanton's son Theodore, his wife, and their baby, mother and daughter left for France. There, Harriot Stanton enrolled in a graduate mathematics program that was not available to women in the United States.

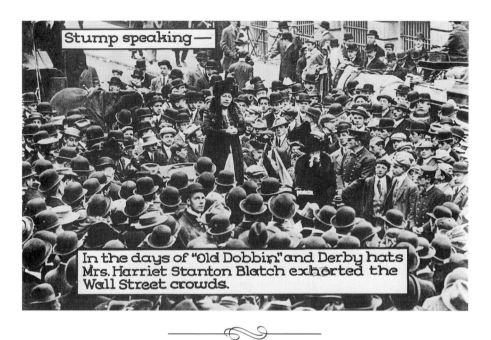

Stump speaking—

In the days of "Old Dobbin" and Derby hats Mrs. Harriet Stanton Blatch exhorted the Wall Street crowds.

Harriot Stanton Blatch, seen here speaking on behalf of women's suffrage to a large crowd, followed in her mother's footsteps to become a famous suffrage leader.

On her mother's sixty-seventh birthday, in November 1882, Harriot Stanton married an Englishman named William Henry Blatch. She had met him while attending graduate school. The newlyweds moved to Basingstoke, a town west of London. Elizabeth Cady Stanton stayed in London. As a reform leader, she spoke to audiences in England and Scotland about such topics as women's suffrage and the advantages of bloomers.

Renewed Friendship

Susan B. Anthony made a trip to England in March 1883. Elizabeth Cady Stanton went to greet her. The two women toured Europe together, making contacts with English suffrage leaders and renewing their old friendship.

In November 1883, Stanton and Anthony made a few visits to say good-bye to friends in London, and the two sailed home. Over the next few years, the two women spent as much time together as possible. Despite numerous disagreements throughout the course of their friendship, Stanton and Anthony always seemed to find a way to become close once again. Both women had strong personalities and opinions that grew more adamant as they got older and often led to disputes between them. Still, their partnership seemed to have a power that could outlast any disagreement.

Early in the spring of 1884, Susan B. Anthony appeared on Stanton's porch, ready to begin work once again on *The History of Woman Suffrage*. The partners remained together, working on the third volume of the work and enjoying each other's company.

Back to the Struggle

Elizabeth Cady Stanton gave the main speech at the NWSA's annual convention in Washington, D.C., in 1885. Her address, "The Limitations of Sex," argued that men and women should be considered equals. The NWSA tried to pass a series of resolutions that centered on the Bible's interpretation of women's role. The organization demanded that Christian churches teach the concept of equal rights being granted to both sexes at creation. The NWSA's efforts paid off. Women who were enthusiastic about the religious idea of equality even began making demands to be made ministers and other officials in Christian churches.

By May 1885, Elizabeth Cady Stanton had moved back to Tenafly. Glad to be home, she was especially happy when Anthony joined her to help complete and publish volume three of *The History of Woman Suffrage* (which covered the struggle to 1885). Eventually, the two would produce a total of six volumes.

A few months after her husband, Henry Brewster Stanton, turned eighty, Elizabeth Cady Stanton celebrated her own seventieth birthday. Friends from the suffrage movement organized a party for her at the home of Dr. Clemence Lozier, one of the first female doctors. That same year, the Stantons also celebrated forty-five years of marriage. Although most historians agree that they did not always share a close relationship, Elizabeth Cady Stanton seemed to care deeply about her husband, who had been one of her first inspirations for entering public life.

In March 1886, when Henry Stanton's health began to fail, the children and grandchildren gathered at his bedside. By fall, his health seemed to be improving. So, in late October 1886, Elizabeth Cady Stanton sailed for England with her granddaughter Nora and niece Hattie. She enjoyed the trip immensely until early January when Hattie brought a message to her aunt. It informed her that Henry Brewster Stanton had died of pneumonia at the age of eighty-one.

Apparently, he had caught cold while waiting in the rain for election returns to be posted.

Elizabeth Cady Stanton did not return to the United States to arrange her husband's funeral. His death seemed to weaken her ties to the United States. In the spring, after spending months depressed over her husband's death, Elizabeth Cady Stanton left England to visit her son Theodore in France. He took his mother on tours of Paris's museums and gardens. By now, Stanton seemed to be more interested in travel and spending time with loved ones. Before long, however, she would find her way back to her life's work.

10

READY TO LEAD THE FIGHT

On the first anniversary of her husband's death, Elizabeth Cady Stanton was ready to rededicate herself to her primary struggle for reform—suffrage for women. At the age of seventy-two, she had now reached what was then considered "old age." Rather than being more dependent on others, however, she was becoming more independent than ever. Without a husband and family keeping her at home, Stanton could now support herself through her writing. Among the works she began at this time were many speeches, articles, and newspaper columns, and a controversial book called *The Woman's Bible*. The only obstacles in her way seemed to be her physical limitations—obesity and failing eyesight.

Rested and Ready

Elizabeth Cady Stanton had written to Susan B. Anthony, promising to return to the United States in time for the March 1888 international women's rights meeting. Stanton lost her courage, however, when faced with the danger and discomfort of an ocean crossing. Anthony warned Stanton that her colleagues would be extremely unforgiving if she failed to attend the meeting. Angry, Stanton cabled a short, rude message to Anthony that said simply, "I am coming."[1]

Seneca Falls Again

Elizabeth Cady Stanton arrived in Seneca Falls, New York, in the middle of a huge blizzard. According to an often-repeated anecdote, Susan B. Anthony became worried when she learned that Stanton had not written a speech to give at the meeting. To prevent problems from arising, Anthony gave Stanton paper and pens and locked her in a room until she had produced a suitable address. Stanton came out after three days with a wonderful speech, up to her usual standard of excellence.

The speech emphasized the importance of uniting different women's groups into one powerful national organization that could fight for women's rights. Elizabeth Cady Stanton welcomed the many foreign delegates who had been invited to help form a "universal sisterhood" of women's rights supporters.[2] On the fortieth anniversary of the first women's rights convention at Seneca Falls, the NWSA created both

an International Council of Women and a National Council of Women.

After the convention, Stanton relaxed, visiting relatives and friends all over the United States. Soon, however, she realized that she was on her own. She no longer had the house in Tenafly, which she had sold after Henry Stanton's death. She returned to New York, looking for a permanent home. Susan B. Anthony offered to let Stanton stay with her. But even though Stanton loved and admired her old friend, she did not want to face Anthony's criticisms about her weight and opinions every day.

Parting Company Again

After the 1888 Seneca Falls convention, Anthony and Stanton not only went in different directions geographically but they also split politically. Anthony began to align with younger, more conservative members of the women's reform movement. She came to believe that the suffrage movement could only succeed if it won the support of middle-class women with traditional values. Many of these women currently opposed the major social changes advocated by suffragists. Most women of the time were very concerned about the family. They believed it was important for women to maintain traditional roles to ensure that children would be raised properly. This attitude was often called the "cult of motherhood." Anthony hoped the suffrage movement could cater to these conservative women and eventually win their support. Stanton, on the other hand, became more radical than ever.

By 1888, women could only vote in certain states, including Wyoming. This is an artist's depiction of women heading to the polls in their first election in Wyoming.

Lucy Stone was one of the best-known leaders of the women's rights struggle, but like Elizabeth Cady Stanton, she never considered herself its unquestioned leader.

Lucy Stone and Susan B. Anthony focused their attention on one cause: women's suffrage. Unlike Stanton, they tended to ignore other issues, such as women's religious and social freedom. Stanton warned Anthony about associating with groups that were closely aligned with organized religion, which, Stanton believed, could harm the goals of the movement.

Despite these vastly different philosophical views, in February 1890, two organizations that had opposed one another for years—the AWSA and the NWSA—met in Washington, D.C., and finally merged, becoming the National American Woman Suffrage Association (NAWSA).

Who would preside over this newly formed group? No one seemed eager to take responsibility. Both Susan B. Anthony and Elizabeth Cady Stanton were nominated for the presidency. Anthony campaigned for Stanton, urging the delegates to give her their votes.[3] Stanton won.

Elizabeth Cady Stanton considered it a great honor to represent the newly united NAWSA. The day after

Mary Church Terrell (1863–1954) picketed the White House on behalf of women's suffrage and spoke out on the rights of black women.

her election, the new president headed back to Europe. Her inaugural speech became her farewell. Stanton's address to the group encouraged suffragists to be open to others' views. She urged NAWSA to accept new members, including African Americans and American Indians. She also demanded that Christian churches make women completely equal, and she asked legislators not to pass any new divorce laws until women were able to vote for or against the measures.

A little more than a year later, Elizabeth Cady Stanton resigned from the NAWSA. She closed her term as president with her speech, "The Solitude of

"The Solitude of the Self"

Stanton wrote that this speech was "the strongest and most unanswerable argument and appeal ever made by mortal pen or tongue for the full freedom and franchise [right to vote] of women."[4] "The Solitude of the Self" pointed to the uniqueness of each individual human soul, which allows every woman to control her own destiny, and urged equal rights because they would allow all human beings to develop according to their own destinies and goals:

> We ask for the complete development of every individual, first, for his own benefit and happiness. In fitting out an army, we give each soldier his own knapsack, arms, powder, his blanket, cup, knife, fork and spoon. We provide alike for all their individual necessities; then each man bears his own burden.[5]

the Self," which she had originally given before the Joint Judiciary Committee of Congress. Cady Stanton always considered this speech "the best thing I have ever written."[6]

Bored with trying to build a successful women's suffrage movement and tired of making the rounds of the conventions, Elizabeth Cady Stanton looked forward to meeting new people in new places. Her only limitation was the fact that she had grown obese and found it hard to move around. Eventually, after suffering two serious falls, Stanton began to use a cane to help her walk, and she hired a maid to help her dress and bathe each day. Most of her daily activities reflected her limitations—reading, writing, playing the piano, entertaining visitors, and taking naps. The older Stanton was no longer the athletic thrill-seeker she had been as a child in Johnstown.

Elizabeth Cady Stanton spent these years in her New York apartment and summers with Libby Miller in Peterboro, New York, or with her children on Long Island. By 1894, she was spending all her time in her apartment. Although she was physically limited, her mind was still sharp.

Stanton was by now too weak to join Susan B. Anthony in lobbying for statewide suffrage in New York. Carrie Chapman Catt and Lillie Blake, two young activists, helped carry on the campaign. Even though the women collected half a million signatures in support of women's suffrage, the state constitutional amendment was defeated by a vote of two to one.

As Stanton and other early suffragists got older, a new generation of leaders, including Carrie Chapman Catt (pictured), took over the struggle.

Despite Elizabeth Cady Stanton's physical problems, Susan B. Anthony did not let her rest for long. Stanton continued to compose speeches that Anthony delivered before conventions and political groups. Stanton also wrote newspaper and magazine articles on a variety of subjects—coeducation, parks and playgrounds for poor children, ending capital punishment, and admitting women into graduate schools.

Two Birthdays

In 1895, the National Council of Women celebrated Susan B. Anthony's seventy-fifth birthday with a banquet. Anthony hoped to have the organization hold a similar celebration for her friend Stanton, but because of Stanton's controversial opinions, Anthony had trouble convincing that group or any other to sponsor such an event.

To honor his mother, it was Theodore Stanton who finally convinced the National Council to help. Susan B. Anthony and other suffragists joined to celebrate Stanton's special day at the flower-filled Metropolitan

Opera House. Stanton's apartment overflowed with gifts and messages.

Stanton was thrilled with the outpouring of support for her, and she did her best to overcome her physical disabilities to attend the grand birthday celebration in her honor. She moved slowly, with the help of a cane and her son Theodore, to a seat at the front of the crowded room. There, despite the fact that she was now nearly blind, she began to read the speech she had prepared for the occasion. She rapidly became too tired to go on, however, and someone else finished reading her address. Just as the National Council had feared, her speech stirred up controversy. Still, Stanton remembered the day fondly, calling it "the dawn of a new day for the Mothers of the Race!"[7]

The Woman's Bible

Despite the criticism she faced, Elizabeth Cady Stanton did not shrink from writing about difficult subjects. Two weeks after her eightieth birthday, she published *The Woman's Bible*. It was Stanton's interpretation of passages in the Bible that referred to women. She expressed a lifetime of anger against organized religion and what it had done to women. Though it was a best-seller, *The Woman's Bible* angered many, especially those among Stanton's fellow suffragists, who feared the work would alienate religious women and men who might otherwise have supported the movement.

Susan B. Anthony tried to persuade Stanton not to publish the controversial work. Stanton refused,

The Woman's Bible

The Woman's Bible was Stanton's way of challenging long-held notions about women's inferiority to men. For many years, ministers had often used the Bible to depict women as weak-willed and dangerous to society. Stanton wanted to prove that women were as valuable as men in the eyes of God.

Throughout her life, Stanton had rebelled against formal religion, especially after her early experiences with the fire-and-brimstone sermons of Charles Grandison Finney. She did not even go to church after her marriage, a very unconventional act for a woman of the nineteenth century. Stanton's own words stated her opinion clearly:

> The Bible teaches that woman brought sin and death into the world, that she precipitated the fall of the race, that she was arraigned before the judgment seat of Heaven, tried, condemned and sentenced. Marriage for her was to be a condition of bondage [slavery]. . . . [8]

eventually publishing two volumes. Almost immediately, Stanton was labeled a heretic (nonbeliever) and condemned, not only by the public but by the NAWSA at its 1896 national meeting.

The controversy over *The Woman's Bible* put Anthony and Stanton on opposite sides again. Despite their public disagreements, however, Elizabeth Cady Stanton still dedicated her autobiography, *Eighty Years and More*, to "Susan B. Anthony, my steadfast friend for half a century."[9] *Eighty Years and More* was published in 1898. It detailed Stanton's life in the women's movement and gave many insights into her personal life, from her childhood to old age.

Later Years

Although Stanton was deteriorating physically, her spirit was strong. Remaining independent, she took every opportunity to give her opinion on subjects as diverse as women's dress and the Spanish-American War. Newspapers continued to print her articles, which kept her name and her radical views before the public, even as she physically retired from the spotlight.

When Susan B. Anthony was in New York City in June 1902, she called her friend's apartment to see if they could get together. When they met, they renewed their friendship as if no separation had occurred, just as they had done many times over the course of a lifetime of working together. As she left, Anthony asked, "Shall I see you again?"

"Oh yes," Stanton answered, "if not here, then in the hereafter. . . ."[10]

The two women made plans to get together on Stanton's eighty-seventh birthday in November. The reunion never happened. Elizabeth Cady Stanton died on October 26, 1902. Her death was attributed to heart failure.

Elizabeth Cady Stanton's death made the front page of *The New York Times* and other major papers

Elizabeth Cady Stanton (left) and Susan B. Anthony enjoyed a partnership and friendship that lasted throughout their lives.

around the nation. Hundreds of condolence letters flooded Cady Stanton's apartment. All were answered with an engraved card signed by her sons and daughters.

Elizabeth Cady Stanton had planned her own funeral. She specified that she should be dressed in normal clothes, not black mourning attire. And, to no one's surprise, she wanted a private ceremony with a woman conducting the funeral.

The service was held at her New York City apartment with Reverend Antoinette Brown Blackwell giving the funeral tribute. On the casket, a photograph of Susan B. Anthony, who had so often spurred Stanton to become a great leader, was placed. The table on which Stanton had written the Declaration of Sentiments, the document that helped start the women's suffrage movement at Seneca Falls back in 1848, stood at the head of the casket. Stanton left life in the same way that she had lived it. She set the agenda for her own funeral just as she had so often worked to dictate the course of the American women's rights movement.

11

A LASTING LEGACY

"We hold these truths to be self-evident: that all men and women are created equal. . . ."1 When Elizabeth Cady Stanton wrote these opening words of the Declaration of Sentiments, she gave a voice to the dreams of three hundred women and men who attended the first women's rights convention in Seneca Falls, New York, in the summer of 1848. With the passing of the Declaration, the fight for women's equality began. And for sixty years, as an author, lecturer, columnist, lobbyist, and philosopher, Elizabeth Cady Stanton tackled inequalities on behalf of women—from voting to wearing bloomers.

Weeks after her death, many American magazines and newspapers paid tribute to the great feminist reformer. At its 1903 national convention, the

Elizabeth Cady Stanton is one of the most respected suffrage leaders. This statue honors three early suffragists—Susan B. Anthony (center), Lucretia Mott (right), and Stanton.

NAWSA held a memorial service in her honor. Susan B. Anthony reminded listeners at the service that, had Stanton been male, with her great intellectual gifts, she might have become a great politician or Supreme Court justice. As she had done many times during their friendship, Anthony stood up for her partner in the women's movement.

Elizabeth Cady Stanton once described her relationship with Anthony: "I am the better writer, she the better critic. She supplied the facts and statistics, I the philosophy and rhetoric, and together we have made arguments that have stood unshaken by the storms of thirty long years. . . ."[2] With Anthony as her partner, Stanton worked her whole life to better the lives of women. Throughout their partnership, Stanton and Anthony held very different opinions, but their friendship withstood even their worst political disagreements. Anthony believed the women's reform movement should focus on one issue, the right to vote. Stanton believed that women's reform should fight for the complete social and religious emancipation of women. Stanton's beliefs were more radical than Anthony's—and the rest of the suffrage leaders of the time.

Neither Stanton nor Anthony (who died in 1906) lived to see the ultimate success of the movement to which they had dedicated their lives. The final struggle for women's right to vote fell into the hands of younger women. Called second-generation suffragists, this new group of women's rights activists were more militant in their demands for suffrage. Under the leadership of the third president of NAWSA, Anna Howard Shaw, they led protest marches and lobbying campaigns to win women the right to vote.

It was these young suffragists who elevated Susan B. Anthony's place in women's history, almost eliminating Stanton, who was still deemed too radical to be embraced by the general movement. Alice Paul, a militant young leader in the women's rights movement, called the proposed women's suffrage amendment to the United States Constitution the Susan B. Anthony Amendment.

Stanton's daughter Harriot Stanton Blatch, herself a prominent suffragist, believed that Susan B. Anthony came to be remembered as the main hero of the suffrage movement because Stanton had lost some of her credibility when she supported radical ideas such as free love and free thought. Later suffrage leaders wanted to make the movement as acceptable and popular as possible in order to win its goal. Stanton's ideas had no place in such a mainstream cause.

What Had They Accomplished?

In spite of their efforts, Elizabeth Cady Stanton, Susan B. Anthony, and other feminist reformers had accomplished little during the nineteenth century to achieve equal rights for women. After almost fifty years of struggling for women's suffrage, only Wyoming, Utah, Colorado, and Idaho had given women the right to vote.

Still, Elizabeth Cady Stanton had had a vision of what was to come. Carrie Chapman Catt, another

Editing the Past

Some published versions of Elizabeth Cady Stanton's history were altered to make her appear less disagreeable to traditional Americans. Historians believe most of the editing of Stanton's autobiography was done by her children Harriot Stanton Blatch and Theodore Stanton. According to historian Elisabeth Griffith, Harriot Stanton Blatch and Theodore Stanton also rewrote some of their mother's letters and destroyed her diary.

Elizabeth Cady Stanton's children not only edited her autobiography, but they deleted and changed some of the work and added fifty pages. When it was first written, Stanton left out anything negative about her marriage, home life, and public life. These inaccuracies included omissions about her family, wrong dates for events, and a clouded memory about any scandals in her life. As a result, the book is sometimes considered a faulty account of her life, though it does give rich insights into her feelings and motivations over the course of her career.

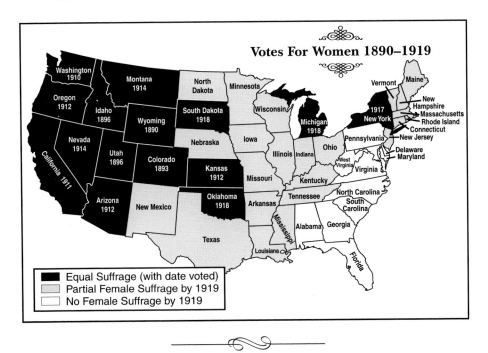

Votes For Women 1890–1919

- Equal Suffrage (with date voted)
- Partial Female Suffrage by 1919
- No Female Suffrage by 1919

This map shows the places that allowed women to vote before the Nineteenth Amendment was passed.

leader in the women's movement, wrote about the new generation of feminists whose work was made easier by the efforts of the older suffrage leaders like Stanton: "Young suffragists who helped forge the last links of that chain were not born when it began. Old suffragists who forged the first links were dead when it ended."[3]

On August 18, 1920, seventy-two years after the first women's rights convention at Seneca Falls, the Nineteenth Amendment to the United States Constitution was ratified. At long last, women all over the United States had won the right to vote.

Future Fights

Discrimination against women did not end with the passage of the Nineteenth Amendment. In the 1960s, several laws were passed to improve women's status. The Equal Pay Act of 1963 required equal wages for men and women who were performing equal jobs. The Civil Rights Act prevented businesses from discriminating against women.

Many retail stores still do not issue independent credit cards to married women. Divorced or single women may still find discrimination in purchasing a car or house and in other areas. Many of the women who are employed still function in clerical, factory, retail sales, and service jobs. The fight for women's equality continues.

Elizabeth Cady Stanton is remembered for her radical beliefs and her tireless efforts to win women's rights.

Many other issues of women's equality remained on the feminist agenda after Elizabeth Cady Stanton's death, and even after passage of the Nineteenth Amendment. A new generation of women carried on the fight Elizabeth Cady Stanton had helped start to secure women's equality in education, in the work force, and in family life. In the continuing struggle for true equality, Stanton's legacy lives on.

CHRONOLOGY

1815—*November 12*: Elizabeth Cady Stanton is born in Johnstown, New York.

1826—Brother Eleazar graduates from Union College, comes home, and dies after a short illness.

1833—Elizabeth Cady graduates from Emma Willard's Female Seminary; After graduation, she spends time at cousin Gerrit Smith's, where she meets her future husband, Henry Brewster Stanton.

1840—*May 11*: Elizabeth Cady marries Henry Brewster Stanton.
June: Attends the World Anti-Slavery Convention in London, where she meets Lucretia Mott.

1848—*July 19–20*: Elizabeth Cady Stanton and four other women hold the first women's rights convention in Seneca Falls, New York.

1851—Meets Susan B. Anthony, who becomes a lifelong friend and partner in the fight for women's equality.

1854—Speaks before the New York state legislature.

1861—Civil War begins.

1863—Stanton and Anthony form the Women's Loyal National League.

1865—Civil War ends.

1868—The first issue of *The Revolution* appears.

1869—Two women's rights organizations are founded: National Women's Suffrage Association (NWSA) with Stanton as president, and the American Woman Suffrage Association (AWSA) headed by Lucy Stone and Julia Ward Howe.

1872—Susan B. Anthony arrested for voting in presidential election.

1881—Stanton and Anthony publish the first volume of *History of Women's Suffrage*.

1882—Elizabeth Cady Stanton moves to Europe for a year.

1883—International Council of Women meets in Liverpool, England, with Anthony and Stanton attending.

1892—Stanton speaks to the United States Congress.

1895—Stanton publishes the first volume of *The Woman's Bible* and celebrates her eightieth birthday at the Metropolitan Opera House in New York City.

1898—Publishes the second volume of *The Woman's Bible*.

1901—Stanton's best-known speeches appear in the *Boston Investigator*.

1902—*October 26*: Elizabeth Cady Stanton dies in New York City.

1920—Seventy-two years after the first women's rights convention in Seneca Falls, New York, the Nineteenth Amendment to the United States Constitution is ratified, giving women the right to vote.

CHAPTER NOTES

Chapter 1. A Promise Fulfilled

1. Elizabeth Cady Stanton, *Eighty Years and More, Reminiscences 1815–1897* (Boston: Northeastern University Press, 1993), p. 145.

2. Ibid., p. 83.

3. Ibid., p. 148.

4. Ibid., pp. 148–149.

5. Geoffrey C. Ward and Ken Burns, *Not for Ourselves Alone: The Story of Elizabeth Cady Stanton and Susan B. Anthony* (New York: Alfred A. Knopf, 1999), p. 39.

6. Ibid., p. 58.

7. Elisabeth Griffith, *In Her Own Right: The Life of Elizabeth Cady Stanton* (New York: Oxford University Press, 1984), p. 55.

8. Ward and Burns, p. 59.

9. Griffith, p. 57.

10. Ward and Burns, p. 41.

Chapter 2. "What a Pity It Is She's a Girl!"

1. Elizabeth Cady Stanton, *Eighty Years and More, Reminiscences 1815–1897* (Boston: Northeastern University Press, 1993), p. 8.

2. Elisabeth Griffith, *In Her Own Right: The Life of Elizabeth Cady Stanton* (New York: Oxford University Press, 1984), p. 3.

3. Stanton, p. 6.

4. Ibid., p. 3.

5. Griffith, p. 4.

6. Stanton, p. 4.

7. Ibid., p. 10.

8. Ibid., p. 11.

9. Ibid., p. 14.

10. Ibid.

Chapter 3. New Shoes to Fill

1. Geoffrey C. Ward and Ken Burns, *Not for Ourselves Alone: The Story of Elizabeth Cady Stanton and Susan B. Anthony* (New York: Alfred A. Knopf, 1999), p. 12.

2. Elizabeth Cady Stanton, *Eighty Years and More, Reminiscences 1815–1897* (Boston: Northeastern University Press, 1993), p. 31.

3. Ibid., p. 32.

4. Ibid., p. 20.

5. Ward and Burns, p. 14.

6. Lois W. Banner, *Elizabeth Cady Stanton: A Radical for Woman's Rights* (New York: HarperCollins Publishers, 1980), p. 12.

7. Stanton, p. 35.

8. Elisabeth Griffith, *In Her Own Right: The Life of Elizabeth Cady Stanton* (New York: Oxford University Press, 1984), p. 17.

9. Louise Bernikow, *The American Women's Almanac: An Inspiring and Irreverent Women's History* (New York: Berkley Books, 1997), pp. 121–122.

10. Griffith, p. 19.

11. Stanton, p. 41.

Chapter 4. A Promise Not to Obey

1. Elizabeth Cady Stanton, *Eighty Years and More, Reminiscences 1815–1897* (Boston: Northeastern University Press, 1993), p. 53.

2. Elisabeth Griffith, *In Her Own Right: The Life of Elizabeth Cady Stanton* (New York: Oxford University Press, 1984), p. 25.

3. Stanton, p. 62.

4. Ibid., p. 59.

5. Lois W. Banner, *Elizabeth Cady Stanton: A Radical for Woman's Rights* (New York: HarperCollins Publishers, 1980), p. 19.

6. Griffith, p. 35.

Chapter 5. Marriage and Motherhood

1. Elizabeth Cady Stanton, *Eighty Years and More, Reminiscences 1815–1897* (Boston: Northeastern University Press, 1993), p. 83.

2. Ibid.

3. Ibid., p. 111.

4. Ibid., p. 120.

5. Lois W. Banner, *Elizabeth Cady Stanton: A Radical for Woman's Rights* (New York: HarperCollins Publishers, 1980), p. 33.

Chapter 6. A Few Years, a Lot of Change

1. Elisabeth Griffith, *In Her Own Right: The Life of Elizabeth Cady Stanton* (New York: Oxford University Press, 1984), p. 50.

2. Ibid., p. 68.

3. Elizabeth Cady Stanton, *Eighty Years and More, Reminiscences 1815–1897* (Boston: Northeastern University Press, 1993), p. 200.

4. Ida Husted Harper, *Life and Work of Susan B. Anthony* (New York: Arno and *The New York Times*, 1969), p. 62.

5. Griffith, p. 74.

6. Stanton, pp. 188–189.

Chapter 7. A Split in the Cause of Equality

1. Louise Bernikow, *The American Women's Almanac* (New York: Berkley Books, 1997), p. 252.

2. Ellen Carol DuBois, ed., *The Elizabeth Cady Stanton–Susan B. Anthony Reader* (Boston: Northeastern University Press, 1992), p. 68.

3. Geoffrey R. Stone, Louis M. Seidman, Cass R. Sunstein, and Mark V. Tushnet, *Constitutional Law*, 2nd ed. (Boston: Little, Brown and Company, 1991), pp. lii–liii.

4. Mari Jo Buhle and Paul Buhle, *The Concise History of Woman Suffrage: Selections from the Classic Work of Stanton, Anthony, Gage, and Harper* (Urbana: University of Illinois Press, 1978), pp. 19–20.

5. Elizabeth Cady Stanton, *Eighty Years and More, Reminiscences 1815–1897* (Boston: Northeastern University Press, 1993), p. 247.

6. DuBois, p. 93.

7. Geoffrey C. Ward and Ken Burns, *Not for Ourselves Alone: The Story of Elizabeth Cady Stanton and Susan B. Anthony* (New York: Alfred A. Knopf, 1999), p. 112.

Chapter 8. On the Road

1. Elisabeth Griffith, *In Her Own Right: The Life of Elizabeth Cady Stanton* (New York: Oxford University Press, 1984), p. 150.

2. Louise Bernikow, *The American Women's Almanac* (New York: Berkley Books, 1997), p. 7.

3. Griffith, p. 168.

Chapter 9. Hellos and Good-byes

1. Elizabeth Cady Stanton, *Eighty Years and More, Reminiscences 1815–1897* (Boston: Northeastern University Press, 1993), p. 329.

Chapter 10. Ready to Lead the Fight

1. Elisabeth Griffith, *In Her Own Right: The Life of Elizabeth Cady Stanton* (New York: Oxford University Press, 1984), p. 192.

2. Ibid., p. 193.

3. Geoffrey C. Ward and Ken Burns, *Not for Ourselves Alone: The Story of Elizabeth Cady Stanton and Susan B. Anthony* (New York: Alfred A. Knopf, 1999), p. 183.

4. Ibid.

5. Elizabeth Cady Stanton, "The Solitude of Self," *The American Reader: Words That Moved a Nation*, ed. Diane Ravitch (New York: HarperPerenial, 1991), p. 202.

6. Ibid., p. 189.

7. Elizabeth Cady Stanton, *Eighty Years and More, Reminiscences 1815–1897* (Boston: Northeastern University Press, 1993), p. 468.

8. Ellen Carol DuBois, ed., *The Elizabeth Cady Stanton–Susan B. Anthony Reader* (Boston: Northeastern University Press, 1992), p. 229.

9. Stanton, *Eighty Years and More*, n.p.

10. Ward and Burns, p. 207.

Chapter 11. A Lasting Legacy

1. Jerome B. Agel, ed., *Words That Make America Great* (New York: Random House, 1997), p. 112.

2. Elisabeth Griffith, *In Her Own Right: The Life of Elizabeth Cady Stanton* (New York: Oxford University Press, 1984), p. 183.

3. Geoffrey C. Ward and Ken Burns, *Not for Ourselves Alone: The Story of Elizabeth Cady Stanton and Susan B. Anthony* (New York: Alfred A. Knopf, 1999), p. 218.

GLOSSARY

abolitionist—A person dedicated to the idea of eliminating slavery.

apprentice—A person who contracts to work without pay for a specified period for an experienced professional, in return for being taught a trade.

cobbling—Shoemaking.

dame school—A school run by a woman in her home that teaches the basics of reading and writing.

delegate—Representative.

feminism—Belief in the equality of the sexes.

heretic—One who goes against the teachings of an established church, often the Roman Catholic Church.

homeopathy—A system that treats disease by giving a patient small doses of medicine or other remedies that would cause symptoms of the disease in a healthy person.

legislator—Law maker.

lyceum—An association that sets up lectures and other public entertainment.

malaria—A bacterial illness transmitted by mosquitoes that can often be deadly.

omnibus—Public vehicle that can carry a large number of passengers.

orthodox—Conventional, traditional, or accepted.

philanthropists—People who give money or time to charity.

Quaker—A member of the religious group called the Society of Friends.

resolution—Formal document or proposal.

taboo—Against the rules of society.

temperance—A movement to ban or limit the use of alcoholic beverages for the good of society.

FURTHER READING

Connell, Kate. *They Shall Be Heard: The Story of Susan B. Anthony & Elizabeth Cady Stanton*. Orlando, Fla.: Raintree Steck-Vaughn Publishers, 1993.

DuBois, Ellen Carol, ed. *The Elizabeth Cady Stanton–Susan B. Anthony Reader*. Boston: Northeastern University Press, 1992.

Fritz, Jean. *You Want Women to Vote, Lizzie Stanton?* New York: Penguin Putnam Books for Young Readers, 1999.

Kendall, Martha. *Susan B. Anthony: Voice for Women's Voting Rights*. Springfield, N.J.: Enslow Publishers, Inc., 1997.

Nash, Carol Rust. *The Fight for Women's Right to Vote in American History*. Springfield, N.J.: Enslow Publishers, Inc., 1998.

Stanton, Elizabeth Cady. *Eighty Years and More, Reminiscences 1815–1897*. Boston: Northeastern University Press, 1993.

Swain, Gwenyth. *The Road to Seneca Falls: A Story about Elizabeth Cady Stanton*. Minneapolis: The Lerner Publishing Group, 1996.

Ward, Geoffrey S., and Ken Burns. *Not for Ourselves Alone: The Story of Elizabeth Cady Stanton and Susan B. Anthony*. New York: Alfred A. Knopf, 1999.

Internet
Addresses

About.com. "Notable Women: Elizabeth Cady Stanton (November 12, 1815 – October 26, 1902)." *Women's History.* 2001. <http://womenshistory.about.com/ library/bio/blstanton.htm>.

The Library of Congress. "Meet Amazing Americans: Elizabeth Cady Stanton." *America's Story from America's Library.* n.d. <http://www.americaslibrary .gov/cgi-bin/page.cgi/aa/stanton>.

National Park Service. "Elizabeth Cady Stanton." *Women's Rights National Historic Park.* n.d. <http://www .nps.gov/wori/ecs.htm>.

National Park Service. "Stanton's Address: Delivered at the Seneca Falls Convention, July 19, 1948." *Women's Rights National Historic Park.* n.d. <http://www .nps.gov/wori/address.htm>.

INDEX